BEN JONSON's
ART

BEN JONSON

BEN JONSON's ART:

Elizabethan Life and Literature as Reflected Therein,

By ESTHER CLOUDMAN DUNN

NEW YORK
RUSSELL & RUSSELL · INC
1963

Causa fuit pater his, qui macro pauper agello
Noluit in Flavi ludum me mittere . . .
Sed puerum est ausus Roman portare, docendum
Artes, quas doceat quivis eques atque senator
Semet prognatos . . .
Ipse mihi custos incorruptissimus omnes
Circum doctores aderat.

Q. Horatii Flacci,
Sermonum Lib. I, 6, ll. 71-82

PREFACE

THE present volume is an attempt to show how the Elizabethan and Jacobean life and literature impressed themselves upon one of the most discerning and keenly critical men of his day, Ben Jonson. With conscious artistry Jonson turned his impressions of the life about him now into corrective satire, now into philosophical comment; so that in order to appraise the value of the reflection of contemporary life which is found in his work one has to understand the colour of Jonson's mind and the purpose of his art. The problem has therefore been twofold: to determine as accurately as possible his view of the time in which he lived; and to show how that time shines through his pages coloured by that view. I have accordingly called the study, *Ben Jonson's Art: Elizabethan Life and Literature as Reflected Therein.*

I undertook this study as a part of the work for the degree of Doctor of Philosophy at the University of London. I carried on my research for two years in London, one year independently and one year as a Foreign Fellow of Bryn Mawr College. I owe much to the inspiration of Professor Caroline F. E. Spurgeon of London University, who was my official supervisor; to Professor Percy Simpson of Oxford, who kindly looked over the historical material which I had collected as a background for my study; and to Professor G. S. Gordon of Oxford, who was my chief examiner for the Doctor's degree.

In the autumn of 1919 appeared Professor Gregory Smith's Life of Jonson in the English Men of Letters Series; and at the same time came the first volume of the definitive edition of Jonson's Works under the editorship of Professors Percy Simpson of Oxford and C. H. Herford of Manchester. I am much indebted to these books.

The privilege of reproducing the two portraits in this volume was graciously granted by George A. Plimpton, Esq., of New York City. The portrait of Jonson was purchased by Mr. Plimpton for his collection recently in England. The portrait of Camden on wood is presumably contemporary and is said to have come from the family house of the Camdens in Kent. Mr. Plimpton obtained it in the Burdett-Coutts sale.

The appendix is an arrangement of the historical and biographical details which were gathered together from various sources. This piece of work threw a good deal of light on the range and emphasis of Jonson's experience among men; and as his personal life furnished the basis on which he selected and arranged the material of his comedies I found such a grouping of historical and biographical data helpful and constructive. I print it in the hope that it may be useful to other students in the same field.   E. C. D.

Northampton, Massachusetts
April, 1925

CONTENTS

ILLUSTRATIONS

NOTE: Ornaments and initials reproduced from Dr. Thomas Lodge's translation
of *Seneca's Works,* as printed by William Stansby, Jonson's printer, London, 1620.

ILLUSTRATIONS

Portrait of Ben Jonson from the Collection of George
A. Plimpton, Esq., now first published . Frontispiece

Note: Ornaments and initials reproduced from Dr. Thomas Lodge's translation
of Seneca's *Works*, as printed by William Stansby, Jonson's printer, London, 1620.

INTRODUCTION

THE picture of life, literture and society which Ben Jonson gives in his writings is full of the colour and atmosphere of London at one of its most fascinating moments. The Court had learned how to be brilliant and lavish and, often, irresponsible. The literary world was open to a great variety of people: university wits and courtiers shared its honours and failures with men of small education and training. Scholarship was pursued in a spirit of adventure and conquest which matched the high enterprise of Raleigh and Drake on the seas. The everyday life which surged through the Strand and Cheapside and overflowed into the narrow lanes and byways, was full of theatrical contrasts: luxury and poverty ran parallel courses. At any moment, by the machinations of someone in authority, a man might pass from one state to the other, from the elaborate silken attire of the Court to the rags and squalor of the debtor's prison. It was a time of sharp distinctions and small compromise.

In fact, the contrasts were becoming so marked that more and more people were questioning them. Society was growing self-conscious and turning its eyes in upon its own code and manner of living. One group of people were protesting against the religious autocracy of the bishops; another group of young satirists scourged the foibles of contemporary society in the manner of Juvenal and enjoyed equally both phases of the process. And the great theatre-going public grew conscious of its influence and made its demands upon the playwright so forcibly that the development of Elizabethan and Jacobean drama is largely a reflection of the changing preferences of public taste. Thus in all the departments of life the reign of authority was weakening. The relationships of classes and groups to one another were examined; when they were faulty they were challenged. The modern world, as we know it, was already well begun.

Into the midst of this exhilarating time, came Ben Jonson. His nature was in accord with this critical view of life. The phenomena of everyday existence, as they passed before his keen observing eye, fell into their places until the world was reduced to categories and the people in it to types. At the same time that Bacon was propounding a new method for science — observation of a number of separate objects and the induction from them of their governing principle — Jonson was applying the same process to human society.

His life and work illustrate the two phases of this process. He had a hearty, flesh-and-blood way of being in the midst of things. When he came abroad to make a good meal among players, his capacity for 'Castalian liquor'[1] was prodigious. He must have been present at many occasions like the supper at the Mitre where the favorite waiter, George, anticipates the well-known order for 'a fat loin of pork to be laid to the fire presently'[2] and the party is interrupted at an awkward moment by the entrance of the constable. He had lived the dare-devil life

---

[1] *E. M. O.*, I, i, p. 71.
[2] *E. M. O.*, V, iv, p. 130 and V, vi, p. 136.

of a professional soldier abroad, had killed an enemy in a duel at home, had stood before the august and unfair courts for judgment, and had fallen in and out of prison with alacrity. He had lived with the wits and braveries of the Court and knew equally well the scholarly retirement of Sir Robert Cotton's library in Westminster and the spacious hospitality of Lord Falkland's country place in Oxfordshire. His experience of the phenomena of human society was as wide and as accurate as a scientist could ask.

For the second part of the process he was equally well fitted. He could at will detach himself from living and reduce his experience to order. If he could roister at the Mitre, he could also, on returning home, write[1]

> Things that were born when nought but the still night
> And his dumb candle saw his pinching throes.

The various phases of existence assumed a pattern when reflected in his orderly mind, and the general trend of life became clear.

It was then his object to give this ordered reflection back to the world, in the hope of clarifying its vision and correcting its follies. As a vehicle, he chose that kind of comedy which Cicero had defined as 'imitatio vitæ, speculum consuetudinis, imago veritatis.'[2] With the licence which has belonged to comedy from the beginning, whether in literature or art, he exaggerated the follies which he meant to correct. His 'speculum consuetudinis' was a kind of magic mirror which slightly distorted the objects it showed, thus heightening their deformity and making more obvious to the spectator their normal proportions.

---

[1] *Poetaster*, Apologetical Dialogue, p. 268.
[2] *E. M. O.*, III, i, p. 105.

The resulting picture of contemporary life in his plays cannot be taken at its face value. It is like the 'perspectives'[1] of pictorial art which were at that time popular. If one looked at them as at a usual picture, they seemed distorted almost beyond meaning. But the artist provided a small hole and by looking through it from a precise angle, one saw the picture restored to its normal proportions.

Jonson gives his readers careful instructions for finding a similar point of view from which the fantasies and exaggerations which move through his pages may be restored again to full reality and flesh-and-blood existence. His prefaces, prologues, inductions and interpretative choruses explain, sometimes with tiresome repetition, 'the springs and mechanism' of his art. He defines his theory of humours, which is, of course, one kind of comic distortion, with academic nicety. Another thing which one must have before determining the point from which to view his 'perspective,' is an understanding of his personality.[2]

---

[1] *Shakespeare's England*, Vol. II, p. 10 and Percy Simpson, ed. of *E. M. I.*, Oxford, 1919, Introduction, p. lviii.

[2] Critics have put much stress upon the supposedly autobiographic characters in his plays. Asper of *E. M. O.*, Crites of *Cynthia's Revels*, and Horace of *The Poetaster*, are taken at their face value as frank revelations of the author's own personality. Nothing could be more absurd and nothing has been more harmful in confusing the world's estimate of him. Though Asper criticises the world and is confident that he can reform it, Jonson does not leave him unchecked in his arrogance. Cordatus points out to him that (*E. M. O.*, Induction, p. 66).

Unless your breath had power
To melt the world and mould it new again,
It is in vain to spend it in these moods.

Yet Jonson's critics disregard this comment; they refuse to see that Cordatus is the creation of the same brain as Asper and that Jonson is, therefore, the very first person to make strictures on Asper's point of view. To take Asper as a serious interpretation of Jonson is wilful perversity.

On this matter he is less capable of informing us and less willing, naturally, to make the effort. What does appear, is that his personality combined a stern morality,[1] a reliance upon reason rather than emotion, with a capacity for fighting and roistering and sharing the gay frivolities of the *beau monde*. This is a rare combination: by a certain power of detachment in his nature he was able at the moments of most whole-hearted absorption in life, to hold himself a bit outside of his experience, to take up a position slightly apart, and from there to ob-

So, too, Crites of *Cynthia's Revels* is often taken literally as Jonson. But the whole play is almost pure allegory. Crites' very name is an abstract quality. Jonson requests the audience again and again to grasp the significance behind his lay figures. Surely he would not thrust a portrait of himself into the midst of these moving shadows. When Mercury praises Crites as 'a creature of a most perfect and divine temper' etc., Cupid mocks his admiration (*Cynthia's Revels*, II, i, pp. 161-2):

Cupid. Slight, I believe he is your minion, you appear to be so ravished with him.

When Mercury, not to be put off, goes on to wish that no wry thought may strike his darling, Cupid adds the final touch of levity:

No, but a straight shaft in his bosom, I'll promise him, if I am Cytherea's son.

Another passage which has been allowed to damn Jonson, is the last line of the Epilogue to *Cynthia's Revels* (*Cynthia's Revels*, Epilogue, p. 204):

By — 'tis good (the play) and if you like 't, you may.

But the lines which precede this show that Jonson is roaring with laughter at his own priggishness. Epilogue says that the author 'jealous how your sense doth take his travails,' has commanded a short and ceremonious speech. Poor Epilogue pauses, confused before the difficult task. He must not kneel and beg the audience's favour; this would anger the author by seeming to distrust his success. If, on the other hand, he approves the play, it will make the author, who has just been condemning self-love, look inconsistent. So he gets even with his difficult master by a wicked fling:

I'll only speak what I have heard him say,
By — 'tis good, and if you like't you may.

The insufferable arrogance goes out of the line when it is read in its context. One should not, indeed, look for a serious portrait of Jonson in his plays. To put one there would be against his theory of comedy and would be uncongenial to his habit of mind.

[1] See Epode, 'Not to know Vice at all,' *Forest*, XI, p. 269.

serve. It is the inevitable position of the comic writer: Meredith places his Comic Spirit overhead, above the ways and acts of men, where it looks 'humanely malign and cast(s) an oblique light on them, followed by volleys of silvery laughter.'[1] Thus in the midst of living, Jonson's comic sense was apart, overhead, looking down upon life and preparing to show it to the world delicately distorted in the oblique light of his personal and artistic creed.

It has been the purpose of the present writer to take his picture of some outstanding phases of contemporary life and to estimate their value as a contribution to the knowledge and understanding of his time. Such subjects have been considered as the influence of the Court and the interrelationship of classes; the problem of dramatic art and the taste of the theatre-goer; the tendencies of the non-dramatic poetry which was then appearing; the methods and aims of contemporary scholarship; the character and significance of everyday life.

In considering these questions it has not been sufficient to take Jonson's material as it stands but to interpret it: to restore it to its normal proportions by bringing to bear upon it the attitude of mind in which it was written and the technical requirements which it had to meet. If the angle of viewing this delicate intellectual 'perspective' has been rightly chosen, the resulting picture of contemporary life, literature and society will add a bit to the interpretation of the past, and to that extent, help to widen the horizon of human experience.

[1] George Meredith, *An Essay on Comedy*, 1897, p. 90.

SYMBOLS AND ABBREVIATIONS

Aubrey   = Aubrey's *Brief Lives*
Case   = *The Case is Altered*
Cyn. Rev. = *Cynthia's Revels*
E. M. I.   = *Every Man in his Humour*
E. M. O.   = *Every Man out of his Humour*
Staple   = *The Staple of News*

The text of Jonson used is that of Gifford-Cunning-ham, in three volumes, Chatto and Windus, London, 1912, except where for special reasons it has been necessary to set it aside. This text includes besides Jonson's own writings the 'Conversations,' the 'Jonsonus Virbius,' etc.; the references to these works are made in the Chatto and Windus edition.

BEN JONSON's ART

CHAPTER I

Jonson and the Court

HE Court played a great part in Jonson's life. To it he owed some of his pleasantest social connections and much of his professional success. It furnished a generous, richly coloured background to soften the austerities of his intellectual life and the restrictions of his material existence. But aside from its value to him personally, he was interested in the Court as one of the shaping factors in the society of his day. A man so thoroughly trained in the classics was bound to recognize the force of formal authority, the great leverage which attaches to position and makes its influence so far reaching. As a child of the Renaissance he would be interested, too, in the question of what constitutes a gentleman and how near the standard of the Court came to answering that question. As a constructive reformer of society, most of all, he was bound

I

to scrutinize and comment upon the ideals and practices of the courtier's life.[1]

Jonson boasted that he had lived for twenty years where he could handle silks and eat 'with the beauties and wits and braveries of the Court,'[2] and the records of his life maintain his boast. For five years[3] (probably from 1602 till 1607) he was counted as a member of the household of Esmé Stuart, Lord Albany. To him Jonson owed succour in a very difficult period of his career.[4] He remembered his obligation in his prosperity and expressed it in the 1616 dedication of *Sejanus*.[5] Albany, as a cousin of James I doubtless commended Jonson to his royal attention when he came to the throne in 1603. Albany must have taken peculiar satisfaction in seeing his protégé grow prominent in the new Court. No doubt he danced with special delight in Jonson's *Hue and Cry after Cupid* at the marriage of Viscount Haddington on Shrove Tuesday, 1608, and sustained the costly honour, three hundred pounds for each masquer,[6] without a murmur.

Whoever first introduced Jonson to royal favour, he was sure to be successful when once he had made the King's acquaintance, for there was much in common in their bluff, downright natures. In the first place, Jonson was of Scotch descent[7] and would be sure to make the

---

[1] The Court with which Jonson was most familiar was the Court of James. For the difference between James's Court and that of Elizabeth, see J. Q. Adams, *A Life of William Shakespeare*, p. 412 seq.

[2] *Underwoods*, LXI, p. 318.

[3] *Conversations*, XIII, p. 482.

[4] *Epigrams*, CXXVII, p. 256.

[5] p. 271.

[6] Edmund Lodge, *Illustrations of British History*, etc., 1791, Vol. III, p. 343, Letter of Rowland White to the Earl of Shrewsbury.

[7] *Conversations*, p. 481.

most of this when other more important people, Sir Robert Cotton for instance,[1] went to such lengths in magnifying their Scottish ancestry, as a compliment to royalty. One must not forget, too, that his grandfather had been a gentleman in the service of Henry VIII[2] and that he took his place at Court as if he belonged there. The community of taste between him and the King ranged from an enjoyment of good wine to an appreciation of poetry and scholarship. When a new royal cellar was built, Jonson wrote some verses in which[3] there is enough classical learning and enough love of wine to suit his royal master, with an added dash of flippancy about mere affairs of state. Bacchus shall lord it at many a royal feast and help to

> . . . gratulate the passage
> Of some well-wrought embassage,
> Whereby he may knit sure up
> The wishèd peace of Europe.

They shared, too, the heavy enjoyment of recondite scholarship. James had written a book on demonology which Jonson used as a source for his *Masque of Queens*. In a footnote on a certain passage,[4] Jonson, with the deferential phrasing of one scholar to another, says: 'His Majesty also remembers the story of the devil's appearance' and makes an illusion to a learned source, of which the King had probably never heard. They were both poets, too, the King the greater of the two in his own esteem and in

[1] Sir Sidney Lee on Sir Robert Cotton in *D.N.B.* Cotton purchased the room in Fotheringay Castle where Mary had been beheaded and had it built into his house at Connington.
[2] *Conversations*, p. 481.
[3] *Underwoods*, LXVII, p. 328. [4] *Masque of Queens*, p. 47.

Jonson's also, if one judges from his fourth epigram.[1] In
this poem his only answer to the charge of flattering the
King's muse would be the exigency of the verse. In any
case he owned a copy of James's *Poetical Exercises at
Vacant Hours*, in the margins of which he has had the
temerity to make numerous corrections of the royal spell-
ing.[2]

Jonson was in the Queen's good graces, too, and wrote
for her the *Masque of Blackness* which was her first essay in formal entertainments. She was so well pleased
that he wrote a second and third entertainment for her
and received from her specific instructions about the
number of masquers and the antimasque.[3] He presented
her with a copy[4] of the first masque with a Latin inscription in his own hand.

Jonson was also a great friend of Prince Henry, who
was only nine when James came to England in 1603 and
died in his eighteenth year, depriving his admiring friends
of their fond hopes that he would some day be one of
England's greatest kings. The 1609 quarto of the *Masque
of Queens*[5] was dedicated by Jonson to him since he had
'graciously commanded the poet to retrieve the particular authorities for his picture of witchcraft' in that
masque, which, Jonson says, he had written 'out of the
fulness and memory of my former readings.' Whether
James had urged the Prince to make this request so that
he might see Jonson's sources on a subject in which he
was much interested, or whether the boy had a precocious

<hr>

[1] p. 225.

[2] *New Poems of James I*, A. F. Westcott, 1911, p. lxxx.

[3] See Jonson's prose introductions to *Beauty* and *Queens*, pp. 10 and 45.

[4] p. 2.   [5] p. 44.

appetite for sheer scholarship (he was then only fifteen), one cannot be sure. But Jonson with charming compliment, took the request at its face value and praised the young inquirer into scholarship for his favour to letters and his interest in poetry.

Jonson and the Prince were almost certainly connected in a more high-spirited adventure and one more suitable to the Prince's years. Henry had in his household at St. James's, one Thomas Coryat, an Oxford man, who put his scholarship in pawn by purveying learned nonsense to the literary and Court society. He was a sort of literary buffoon whose sugar-loaf head and face which, as Fuller's shrewdly remarks, 'shewed memory and fancy but no common sense,' amused the young Henry. When his book on continental travel was coming out (circ. 1610-11), Jonson 'apparently at the desire of Prince Henry,' undertook[1] to arrange 'that immense farrago of burlesque testimonies to the author's merit' which accompanied the first edition. Coryat probably solicited most of these verses from the literary people of the time, who saw in the invitation an opportunity to be witty at his expense. Jonson and the Prince must have grown very merry over the compilation. It was almost certainly Jonson's hand which wrote the characterization of Coryat[2] which precedes the commendatory verses. 'He (Coryat) is an engine wholly consisting of extremes, a Head, Fingers and Toes. For what his industrious toes have trod, his ready fingers have written, his subtle head dictating.' In the whole passage Jonson parodies his own

[1] J. B. Nichols, *Progresses and Processions of James I*, 1828, II, p. 400. Also Jessop *D. N. B.* on Coryat.

[2] Thos. Coryat, *Crudities*, Printed by W. S.: London, 1611, (no pagination).

analytic style in characterizing people, and makes delicious nonsense. Perhaps he was present when Coryat made his presentation speech, accompanying the gift of the[1] volume to the Prince and begged him to allow 'this tender-feathered redbreast' (the presentation copy of the *Crudities* is bound in scarlet velvet) to make 'his cage in your Highness's study.'[2] Jonson's romantic side was touched, too, by the great future which seemed to lie just ahead of this charming boy; in the *Speeches for Prince Henry's Barriers* which he wrote in January, 1610-1611, he recalls with delicate appropriateness the spirit of England's early heroic days in Arthur and the figures of chivalry.

It is pleasant to think of Jonson in the midst of the great figures of the Court. He knew and shared their tastes in wine, poetry and jollity; and the romance of royalty, its gorgeous potentialities, were never far from his mind. One looks in vain in the fleeting glimpses of his actual life there, for the sights and experiences which must have formed the basis of those innumerable portraits of the vicious, superficial courtling whom he handles so mercilessly in his plays. The Court was a two-headed affair for him. He was wonderfully quick to see and appreciate its great qualities: he loved its gracious urbanities and none knew how to show them to better advantage; for his masques and entertainments were devised to display the Court in its most brilliant moments. But when he saw a certain contingent of court society

---

[1] Ms. letter of Coryat from Bowe Lane, bound into presentation copy of *Crudities*, now in British Museum. Printed by W. S.: London, 1611. Bound in red velvet.

[2] *Coryats Crambe*, London, Wm. Stansby, 1611, in an unpaged section of 'Certain Orations.'

despising its high standards and neglecting the basis of its greatness, he turned to satiric comedy to punish the thing that he loved and restore it to its beauty.

How much he loved it and how sympathetically he appraised its gentilities, one can see from a study of his entertainments. When Queen Anne and Prince Henry were on their way from Edinburgh to assume their royal state in London, they spent a week-end at Sir Robert Spencer's country place, Althorpe. Jonson was selected to devise an entertainment for the guests. He never, I think, wrote more charmingly than in this little dramatic idyll which he called *The Satyr*. It has a delicacy of touch, a piquancy of handling; it shows how well he knew the taste of the choice, gentle group gathered there. In constructing it, he had clearly in mind the plan of the grounds at Althorpe, the gardens and drives, the bits of woodland which surrounded this hospitable country seat. He was evidently present for the[1] performance and no doubt a welcome guest, too. The opening stage direction suggests the atmosphere; 'A satyr, lodged in a little spinet (copse of young wood) by which her Majesty and the Prince were to come, at the report of certain cornets . . . advanced his head above the top of the wood, wondering, and with his pipe in his hand, began.' He darted out of the shrubbery, gazed boldly at the royal pair, then 'ran into the wood again and hid himself, whilst to the sound of excellent soft music, that was concealed in the thicket, there came tripping up the lawn a bevy of fairies.' The whole scene comes before one with these conjuring words. The new queen was perhaps now seeing for the first time

[1] See prose explanations in *Satyr*, p. 576.

that exquisite delicacy of imagination, combined with sprightly joy in life, which was one of the precious gifts which Elizabethan England had to give to its new mistress. Beside her stood the boy who probably felt that the highest moment in the entertainment was when a brace of deer were let loose from the covert 'and as fortunately killed, as they were meant to be, even in the sight of her Majesty.'

Among the noble and fair guests were several with whom Jonson would have more to do in later years. There was Sir John Spencer's daughter, Alice,[1] who as the Countess of Derby, danced in Jonson's *Masque of Blackness*. She married as her second husband, Lord Keeper Edgerton, who played such a part in the life of Jonson's friend, John Donne. Lady Anne Clifford who came thither with her mother, left an account of her stay in her diary.[2] She missed the Saturday performance, which is a great loss to us as well as to her, and arrived on Sunday which 'was kept with great solemnity, there being an infinite number of lords and ladies.' She was later a dancer in both his masques of *Beauty* and *Queens*.

In the character of the simple, straightforward Sir Robert Spencer, the lord of Althorpe, Jonson found that type of courtier in whom he gloried and with whom he contrasted the wantonly frivolous courtling. He wished the Queen to see from the lines of his play that her host had

> Little of the nicety
> In the sprucer courtiery

---

[1] Nichol's *Progresses and Processions*, Vol. I, p. 488.

[2] *Lives of Lady Anne Clifford*, etc. Harl. Ms. 61777, ed. Roxburghe Club, 1916, and Nichol's *Progresses and Processions*, Vol. I, p. 174.

that

> He can neither bribe a grace
> Nor encounter my lord's face
> With a pliant smile and flatter.[1]

But he is loyal to the core and full of staunch virtues, friendly and beloved by the country people round about. They come thronging to Althorpe on Monday morning to do[2] homage to their new Queen and are sure of a kindly welcome in a place where the obligation of the great house to the surrounding tenantry could not be forgotten.

Another pleasant occasion was the performance of Jonson's *Penates*. It was acted in the garden of Sir William Cornwallis at Highgate, on May Day, 1604, for the visit of the King and Queen. The text shows not only that Jonson knew the place well but that he knew intimately the people who met there. After a welcoming speech,[3] 'the Penates lead them through the house into the garden' where later Pan offers them drink from a fountain running wine. His shrewd personal remarks as he hands about the glasses show how well Jonson knew the peculiarities and interests of each guest. No doubt these hits caused much merriment and altogether it must have been a pleasant party for that courtly company, who strayed through garden paths on a fresh May day with a poet steeped in classic lore to turn their pretty English landscape into a graceful Roman tableau.[4]

---

[1] *Satyr*, p. 575.   [2] *Satyr*, p. 576.   [3] *Penates*, p. 579.

[4] 'Under yon purslane tree,' says Mercury, 'stood sometime my cradle . . .'. Here for her month yearly, delicate May keeps state; and from this mount takes pleasure to display these valleys, yond lesser hills, those statelier edifices and towers, that seem enamoured so far off, and are reared on end to behold her, as if their utmost object were her beauties.' p. 580.

Jonson's figure was equally familiar in the banqueting room at Whitehall on occasions of Court revelry. Pory, writing to Sir Robert Cotton in January, 1605-1606[1] about the masque of *Hymen* for the marriage of Essex and Frances Howard, says: 'Both Inigo, Ben and the actors, men and women, did their parts with great commendation . . . . Before the sacrifice could be performed, Ben Jonson turned the globe of the earth, standing behind the altar.' What figure he made standing behind Hymen's altar, amid saffron-robed youths and maids garlanded with roses, is difficult to imagine. But the distinguished author's appearance was a matter to be noted in Pory's account. On another occasion at Court he behaved with quite as much prominence but not with equal credit. He had gone with his friend, Sir John Roe, to see the court performance of Daniel's *Vision of Twelve Goddesses*. They were ushered out from the masque[2] before its conclusion by the Lord Chamberlain, Lord Suffolk. One imagines that Jonson made himself unpleasantly critical of the performance and disturbed its progress.

When one considers the personal and professional relations which Jonson had with royalty and the Court, one realizes that the distinguished names which appear in his dedications and more especially in his non-dramatic poems, are more than the formal addresses by which an author pays tribute to the great people of his day. Beneath the conventional formality of such verse, there is ample reflection of his graceful familiarities with the people of the Court. One sees that he was as engaging and

---

[1] *Court and Times of King James*, 1848, I, pp. 41-42.
[2] *Conversations*, XI, p. 477.

attractive as he was bluff and downright. On one occasion, his friend, the Countess of Bedford, neglected to
send him the promised gift of a buck and he teased her for
her negligence in graceful verse. He had complained
roundly to her of some lordly acquaintance who had
promised him a buck and then forgotten it, and we may
imagine how the Countess, there and then, promised him
the very finest buck in her forest, while she scolded the
forgetful lord and called herself more discerning. Thus,
says the poet,[1]

> Straight went I home; and there most like a poet
>   I fancied to myself what wine, what wit
> I would have spent; how every Muse should know it,
>   And Phoebus' self should be at eating it.
> O madam, if your grant did thus transfer me,
>   Make it your gift. See whither that will bear me.

Jonson wickedly enjoyed taunting the Countess for be-
having as badly as the unfortunate lord; and when he
went to Scotland he repeated the poem to Drummond
with tremendous relish.[2]

Jonson's wit is not slow when gentle ladies are in-
volved. The Earl of Pembroke, that imaginative patron
who gave Jonson an annual gift of twenty pounds for
books,[3] one day fell into an argument with his lady over
a chance remark, that women were men's shadows. They
both appealed to Jonson, who was present. It was a delicate situation for him but, as he told Drummond, 'he[4]
affirmed it (the Earl's saying) true; for which my lady
gave a penance to prove it in verse.' Thereupon Jonson

---

[1] *Epigrams*, LXXXIV, p. 241.
[2] *Conversations*, p. 473.
[3] Gregory Smith, *Ben Jonson*, p. 40, and *Conversations*, p. 483.
[4] *Conversations*, p. 485.

wrote a song in which he cleverly maintains the Earl but
is sufficiently chivalrous to please any lady:[1]

> Follow a shadow, it still flies you,
>   Seem to fly it, it will pursue:
> So court a mistress, she denies you,
>   Let her alone, she will court you.
> Say are not women truly then
>   Styled but the shadows of us men?

Even in his acceptance of patronage, Jonson behaves
as an equal, not as a social inferior. In writing to thank
Sir Edward Sackville, Earl of Dorset for some benefac-
tion, he says:[2]

> . . . . though my fortune humble me to take
> The smallest courtesies with thanks, I make
> Yet choice from whom I take them . . .

He graciously confesses that these are most acceptable
when

> The memory delights him more, from whom
> Than what, he hath received . . .

Jonson had the true aristocratic feeling and took his place
in the Court, as among his equals. It was the recognition
of this fact which so angered some of his fellow playwrights.

But aside from reflecting his personal relationships to
the Court, Jonson's non-dramatic poems, *The Epigrams,*
Underwoods and *Forest,* give an interesting suggestion
of his attitude to the Court as a factor in society, and fore-
shadow the point of view which appears in his comedies.
He summarizes the impotence of the courtier whose emp-

[1] *Forest*, VII, p. 267.
[2] *Underwoods*, XXX, p. 299.

ty life holds neither good nor ill, in a biting epigram which concludes with the line:

> Good Lord, walk dead still.[1]

He shows the wrong use of social position, in some verses where a robber is released from his charge by the mere request of a courtier.[2] The foibles of court fashion, such as the wearing of silk,[3] the use of expensive perfumes,[4] are harshly treated. But side by side with this carping, goes a more constructive view. Jonson admired tremendously the great profession of statesmanship, its far reaching power and effectiveness; behind the useless troop of court idlers, he was always conscious of the great figures who held the Empire in trust. His idea of real aristocracy, which no man worshipped more, is always based upon nobility of feeling, sense of obligation and not upon external position. In writing to Sir William Jephson, he says:[5]

> Thou wert the first mad'st merit know her strength
>
> . . . .
>
> That blood not minds, but minds did blood adorn
> And to live great was better than great born.

In addresses to various prominent people, Salisbury upon the accession of the Treasurership to him, Suffolk, Sir Horace Vere, and Egerton, the Lord Chief Chancellor, Jonson[6] repeats the idea that virtue alone should be the basis of preferment in public life and is so, in these cases which he chooses to commend. In contrast to these men,

---

[1] *Epigrams*, XI, p. 226. [2] *Epigrams*, VIII, *ibid*.
[3] *Epigrams*, XV, p. 227. [4] *Epigrams*, XIX, p. 228.
[5] *Epigrams*, CXVI, p. 253.
[6] *Epigrams*, LXIV, LXVII, XCI, LXXIV, pp. 237, 238, 243, 239.

Jonson places the young nobles who solely through their social position hold some minor post in the affairs of state. Their only qualification is a glib superficiality which covers their bottomless ignorance. He attacks them with spirit in an epigram called *The New Cry:*[1]

> Ere cherries ripe! and strawberries! be gone,
> Unto the Cries of London I'll add one.
> Ripe Statesmen, Ripe! they grow in every street
> At six and twenty, ripe.
>
> . . . .
>
> They know the states of Christendom, not places;
> Yet they have seen the maps and bought them, too,
> And understand them as most chapmen do.

He returns to the same theme in his portrayal of Sir Politic Wouldbe in *Volpone.* In a brief glance at his poems, his adverse criticism is so much greater in proportion and more keenly expressed, than his commendation, that one is likely to regard him as an enemy of the Court, while, as we have seen, he was devoted to it and keenly alive to its great qualities.

In the non-dramatic poems where he does not adopt a satiric vein we turn disappointedly away and call him dull; we miss the poignancy and keen intellectual vivacity which characterize his comedies and his best epigrams. Yet the substance of these poems is worthy of consideration. He is frankly moral in commending those people of nobility who meet the obligations of their position and set a virtuous example before the world. He praises the country houses of Penshurst and Durance where the realities of life are valued. He commends the great seat of the Sidneys because[2] it is not built 'to envious show of

[1] *Epigrams,* XCII, p. 243.
[2] *Forest,* II, 262 seq.

touch (a kind of expensive stone) or marble.' After a pretty picture of its hospitality and diversions, he pays it a high compliment in saying that while other country houses may surpass it in elaborateness, yet here the fulness of life is experienced. Lords of more pretentious and fashionable houses have merely built, 'but thy lord dwells.' No one understood the depth and richness of real living better than Jonson; and it is the lack of this, the throwing away of golden opportunity, which he laments in the frothy life of the Court. In writing of Sir Robert Wroth's country place of Durance, Jonson[1] particularly notes that although Sir Robert lives so near the Court, he passes his time in the quiet pursuit of simple pleasures. He scorns masquings, those 'short braveries of a night' where the expense is so great in proportion to the return. One is surprised to find Jonson taking this attitude toward masques; yet it only serves to illustrate how squarely he looked at things, even those things in which he might be excused for having a prejudiced point of view. The temper of both these country pieces has been called 'reminiscent of Horace,'[2] especially in the Ode, 'Beatus ille qui procul negotiis.' But it is not merely a reminiscence. The same sort of costly frivolity obtained in the Roman Emperor's and the English James's Court, and both poets were quick to feel it and to find comfort in the realities of country life.

I have said that many of these non-dramatic poems show Jonson's morality, untouched by satiric point; and it is interesting to see precisely what the quality of that morality is. In his *Farewell to the World by a Gentle-*

[1] *Forest*, III, p. 264. [2] Gregory Smith, *Ben Jonson*, 1919, pp. 234-5.

woman, Virtuous and Noble,[1] he pictures the cold surfeit
of worldly pleasures, from which the lady turns to find
support in her own spirit:

> No, I do know that I was born
> To age, misfortune, sickness, grief,
> And I will bear these with that scorn
> As shall not need thy false relief.
>
> . . . .
>
> And make my strengths, such as they are,
> Here in my bosom and at home.

One recalls the lines in Wordsworth's *Happy Warrior,*
so similar in content yet so different in emphasis:

> Who doomed to go in company with pain
> And fear and bloodshed, miserable train,
> Turns his necessity to glorious gain.

It is the lack in Jonson of the power to turn the necessity
of evil into glorious gain which makes him so much less
happy and inviting in his attitude toward life than either
Wordsworth or Shakespeare. For him there was no way
of transmuting evil into good. The only way to treat evil
was to point it out frankly or satirically, maintain a
strictly hostile attitude to it and start anew. With this
point of view, it is fortunate that Jonson chose more often
the satiric rather than the frank treatment of evil; for the
frank expression of aversion to evil is bound to be melodramatic, if scornful, and sentimental, if meek, and Jonson
shows both these qualities when he leaves his satiric vein.
The gentlewoman who takes her farewell with the words,
"False world, good-night!"[2] is somewhat theatrical and

---

[1] *Forest,* IV, p. 266.
[2] *Forest,* IV, p. 266.

the Lady Albany whom Jonson commends for forsaking the wicked world to practice wifely arts, is[1] flat and dull.

On the other hand, when one turns to the 'comically satiric' handling of the Court and fashionable society in his plays, the splendid appropriateness of comedy for Jonson is apparent. Jonson's mind must get to the elements which made up life and he enjoyed too much the intellectual process of analysis, to deny it. But intuitively at least, he must have realised that the sum of his analysis would not make life again, that some magic element had gone in the process. It was only when he used his separate elements to emphasize the existence of a folly or drive home its futility that his analysis of human nature was justified. Thus he differentiates the outstanding weaknesses of the Court and exaggerates them with delicacy of touch, to open the eyes of a too thoughtless group to its own importance and the neglect of its splendid opportunities.

In 1601 he devoted a whole play to the delicate distortion of Court life and became so preoccupied with his undertaking that plot and character are well night forgotten. He dedicates *Cynthia's Revels* to 'The Special Fountain of Manners, the Court':[2]

Thou are a bountiful and brave spring, and waterest all the noble plants of this island. In thee the whole kingdom dresseth itself and is ambitious to use thee as her glass. Beware then thou render men's figures truly, and teach them no less to hate their deformities than to love their forms (Note his interest in form and the deviation from it and recall the peculiar corrective method of his 'humours' which by distorting life recall its normal form): for to grace there should

[1] *Forest*, XIII, p. 273.
[2] *Cynthia's Revels*, Dedication, p. 143.

come reverence; and no man can call that lovely which is not also venerable. It is not powdering and perfuming . . . that converteth to a beautiful object; but a mind shining through any suit, which needs no false light, either of riches or honour, to help it . . .

Jonson was of course, familiar with the nice problem of the relationship of spirit to outward form which Plato had propounded and with which, especially in its application to manners and conduct, Renaissance writers are often concerned. Spenser has expressed it in his *Hymn to Heavenly Love and Beauty:*

For soul is form and doth the body make.[1]

In much of the Court society of his day Jonson saw the absolute denial of this principle. There the stress was so often put upon externals while the central principle of true gentility was not comprehended. It was this which appalled him.

One of the ways in which he judges the Court most surely and touches its superficiality to the quick is in showing the sort of appreciation which it gave to scholarship, poetry and the theatre. It was fashionable at Court to affect these things; and there are many instances in Jonson's comedies where a courtier steals to some obscure poet or scholar in a by-street to get scraps of French or Italian, or verses with which to win his lady's favour.[2] Madame Philautia, the very mint of fashion, has 'a good superficial judgment in painting and would seem to have so in poetry.'[3] Among the lighter bits of that dark comedy, *Volpone,* is the spirited description of Lady Would-be's call upon the Fox who suffers from the empty talk of

---

[1] 'An Hymne in Honour of Beautie,' *Works of Spenser,* Ed. R. Morris, 1910, p. 597.
[2] *Cynthia's Revels,* II, i, p. 163; III, i, p. 165; III, iii, p. 170.   [3] *Id.,* II, i, p. 163.

this fashionable blue-stocking. From her tongue the names of all the poets from the beginning of time fall trippingly, accompanied by a neat, superficial judgment on each:

> . . . . . . Montaignié (sic)
> He has so modern and facile a vein
> Fitting the time and catching the Court ear!
> Your Petrarch is more passionate, yet he
> In days of sonneting, trusted them much.
> Dante is hard and few can understand him
> But for a desperate passion, there's Aretine,
> Only his pictures are a little obscene.[1]

The joy with which Jonson makes her mispronounce the names of her poets and confuse her tags of criticism, is probably retaliation for many a wearisome conversation in which a pretty and empty-headed lady had tried to talk learnedly to him.

The way in which the fashionable people could impose their opinions upon an audience at the theatre was important for the course of the drama. He satirizes their conservative, conventional taste.[2] They like the old-fashioned revenge plays, such as Kyd's *Spanish Tragedy,* and cannot bear to have them brought up to date, even when Jonson, himself, with surprising imaginative art, makes remarkable additions. The corpulent middle-aged conservative is only pleased with a dramatic style which is contemporary with the cut of his doublet, now twenty years out of fashion. Then there are those 'civet wits' that 'know no other learning than the price of satin and velvet' yet feel the right to censure a play 'as desperate-

---

[1] *Volpone*, III, ii, p. 365.
[2] *Cynthia's Revels*, Induction, p. 147.

ly as the most profound critic in the house, presuming his clothes should bear him out in it.' Another, failing the wit to comprehend the lines, calls it all 'fustian' and has done with it. Thus fashionable society at the play claims the right to comment and affect public opinion, but lacks the discernment and wit to judge rightly.

Conversation, too, which to Jonson was one of the most precious means of intellectual enjoyment,[1] is for the frivolous element at Court a matter of fashion. It[2] must be well larded with foreign phrases and with reminiscences of foreign travel. It must affect an interest in the public issues of the day, or mention the latest benefactions of a fashionable charity-worker. The superficial bandying of 'cultural' topics was as great a humbug in his fashionable world as it is in ours.

Crites summarizes his reasons for scorning Court society. He regrets the waste of energy and brains in the pursuit of 'these outward and effeminate shades.' Instead of the practice of a

> . . . . . Forced look,
> An antic gesture or a fustian phrase,

he would have these people study

> the native frame of a true heart,
> An inward comeliness of bounty, knowledge,
> And spirit that may conform them actually
> To God's high figures . . . [3]

As a good student of Plato, or, leaping the centuries, of Castiglione and the Renaissance ideal, Jonson knew that the gentle heart is the true fountain whence nobility

---

[1] Cf. Master Francis Beaumont's Letter to Ben Jonson, G. C., Vol. I, p. cxiv.
[2] *Cynthia's Revels*, I, i, p. 154. [3] *Cynthia's Revels*, V, ii, p. 195.

springs and that much of the professed gentility of the Court did not come from this source. This was what concerned him.

His actual connection with the Court is reflected in an interesting way in the plays written by and against him in the 'stage quarrel.' In the *Satiromastix* Dekker's chief point of attack on Jonson is his acquaintance with the nobility.[1] He makes Horace (i.e. Jonson) accept payment in return for poems which he writes for gentlemen. Horace cultivates the society of young gallants and counts upon their support in case a play should be launched against him. Though Dekker admits it but grudgingly, he does testify to Jonson's success with the Court. Tucca says:[2]

Horace (i.e. the historic Horace) did not wriggle and screw himself into great men's familiarity, impudently, as thou dost: nor wear the badge of gentleman's company, as thou dost thy taffety sleeves, tacked too (sic) only with some points of profit.

No doubt Dekker exaggerates Jonson's efforts to get into favour in high places; but one may be sure that he loved the world of influence enough to do his share in commending himself to it, not in a fawning way but out of a clear-eyed appreciation of its quality. Besides, he had a very human enjoyment in being prominent, as Sir Vaughan shows in the *Satiromastix:*[3]

Sir Vaughan. Moreover, you shall not sit in a gallery, when your comedies and interludes have entered their actions, and there make vile and bad faces at every line, to make gentlemen have an eye to you . . . Besides, you must foreswear to venture on the

---

[1] *Satiromastix and Poetaster*, ed. J. H. Penniman. *Satiromastix* I. ii, p. 285; II, ii, p. 312; I, ii, p. 286. [2] *Ibid.*, V, ii, p. 388. [3] *Ibid.*, V, ii, p. 380.

stage when your play is ended and to exchange courtesies and com-
pliments with gallants in the Lord's room, to make all the house rise
up in arms and cry, That's Horace (Jonson), that's he, that's he,
that's he, that pens and purges humours and diseases.

Thus Jonson, the relentless purger of humours, indulged
an innocent foible of his own which he patently displayed
for his enemies' attack. Sir Vaughan also shows what a
pleasant expansiveness of manner came upon him when
he dined abroad in fashionable company.[1]

When you sup in taverns amongst your betters, you shall swear
not to dip your manners in too much sauce, nor at table to fling
epigrams . . .

Every lover of Jonson owes much to Dekker for exposing
him at a moment of such engaging weakness.

Dekker makes a more serious charge when he says that
Jonson abuses the privilege of gentle society by making
'scald and wry-mouth jests' upon it.[2] But Jonson declares in the *Poetaster*[3] that he has never been known to
wrong or tax a friend. He did not feel that his satire of
the Court was personal; in fact he had a horror of this
sort of thing. He repeats over and over in his prologues
and dedications that he is as far removed as possible from
personal attack. We must believe that he was sincere in
his protestations; it would weaken the far-reaching effect
of satire to limit its application to any individual. Furthermore, Jonson's conception of friendship[4] and his real
pleasure in his personal connection with the Court, would
prevent him from misusing it.

Dekker also taxes him with maintaining that 'arro-

---

[1] *Ibid.*, V, ii, p. 391.'   [2] *Ibid.*   [3] *Poetaster*, V, i, p. 258.
[4] *Underwoods*, LVI and LXIV, p. 314 and p. 325.

gance, impudence and ignorance are the essential parts
of a courtier."[1] Jonson would be the first to admit that
he did present these qualities as characteristic of many
courtiers, but that they were essential to the courtier, he
did not and could not believe. His preoccupation with
the foibles of the court was founded upon a conviction of
its real worth. He always relies upon the sound element
in the Court to support him in his attack. In *Cynthia's
Revels,* Crites confides to Mercury that he is troubled
about this attack he has been making on the frivolous
courtlings:[2]

> *Crites.* The offence will be returned with weight on me
> That am a creature so despised and poor,
> When the whole Court shall take itself abused
> By our ironical confederacy.

To his fear Mercury gives substantial comfort:

> *Mercury.* You are deceived. The better race in Court
> That have the true nobility called virtue,
> Will apprehend it as a grateful right
> Done to their separate merit, and approve
> The fit rebuke of so ridiculous heads.

In other passages, too, Jonson expected the best part of
the Court to uphold him. He was merely correcting the
foibles in an institution mainly good, not being a destructive scorner and contemner of the time.

He cleverly points out the folly of basing nobility upon
externals, by showing what things seem essential to the
social aspirant in order to be admitted to the coveted circle. In the *Alchemist,* Dame Pliant, a rich young widow
of nineteen but just come up to town, has settled to the

[1] *Satiromastix*, IV, iii, p. 362. [2] *Cynthia's Revels,* V, p. 183.

serious business of learning the fashion and of marrying again to nothing less than a knight.[1] She hesitates to consult an alchemist because she will be talked about and such gossip will hurt the prospects of her remarriage. It is a demure thought and does her simple country life credit; but she learns, to her confusion, that in town, gossip about a widow is her chief recommendation. Her brother Kastril, too, that 'gentleman newly warm in his land,' who has come to London 'to learn to quarrel and to live by his wits,' has many surprises in store for him. When he learns that[2] he must frequent ordinaries, he hesitates with a wise provincial conservatism. There will be gaming and tricks there, such as will spend a man. But that way lies the path of fashion and he must tread it. The vicious futility of fashionable pastimes and the unsavory breath of scandal fit strangely with these fresh country figures, who find that the way to social success lies through the acquirement of polite vices. The gentility upon which true nobility is based, does not cross their minds. It is still talked about, but without meaning. When Dol Common, dressed like a great lady, goes to beguile Sir Epicure Mammon, she does not forget to speak pretty platitudes like this:[3]

> Sir, although
> We may be said to want the gilt and trappings,
> The dress of honour, yet we strive to keep
> The seeds and the materials.

As the only marks of a lady which Dol possesses are her trappings, the point is shrewdly made. Thus the social

[1] *Alchemist*, II, i, p. 35.   [2] *Ibid.*, III, ii, p. 43.
[3] *Ibid.*, IV, i, 47.

climber struggles only to make his externals acceptable
and the sentiments of gentility in the mouths of Dol
Commons echo strangely and from afar.

Holding, as he did, so high a view of the responsibility
and dignity of statesmanship, nothing in the whole range
of Court deficiencies annoyed him more than to have
trivial people concerned with affairs of state. In Sir Politic Would-be he pictures the futile nobleman who wishes
to be thought great in matters of state and poses as close
to the British Embassy in Venice. He utters his platitudes with a pompous assurance which makes delicious
reading

> Sir (he says to Peregrine) to a wiseman all the world's his soil,
> It is not Italy, nor France, nor Europe
> That must bound me if my fates call me forth.[1]

His fate in this particular instance, is Lady Would-be's
humour to learn the Italian language and fashion, while
he hangs onto the followers of the lord ambassador and
gathers such bits of information as, from his point of
view, might shake a kingdom. When he asks Peregrine
for home news from England, he is concerned with idle
scraps — that a raven has built in a royal ship, that por-
poises appeared above one of London's bridges, portend-
ing dark things. He imagines he is the victim of elaborate
systems of espionage and feels he runs a daily risk of having his important mail intercepted. When Peregrine
plays a practical joke upon him and has him searched for
supposedly plotting against the government, he admits
that the apparently important notes on statecraft are
really only passages from playbooks. As for his treason-

---

[1] *Volpone*, II, i, p. 349.

ous conversation,

> Sir, I but talked so[1]
> For discourse' sake merely.

Although Sir Politic is one of the relieving elements in the sinister comedy of *Volpone*, yet through the knight's amusing futilities, Jonson strikes boldly at inconsequential people of fashion who flirt with affairs of state.

In *Epicoene* Jonson adds Clerimont to his gallery of fashionable young gallants and portrays another social aspirant in Sir Amorous La Foole who is well touched off for his eagerness to know prominent people, and gives an amusing account of the ancient lineage of the Foole family. But as a whole, *Epicoene* seems to lack the moral zeal, the constructive scorn, which Jonson put into his earlier satire of the Court. He marks certain follies and stops there. He seems less hopeful than in the earlier days of *Every Man out of his Humour* and *Cynthia's Revels,* when the spectacle of the Court was newer to him. In the *Alchemist* (1610) he shows the outsider who grasps eagerly for the externals of fashionable life; but the Court is no longer his chief concern. *Bartholomew Fair* is entirely beyond the pale of the Court, for as Grace Well-born remarks, 'there's none goes thither of any quality or fashion.'[2] In *The Devil is an Ass,* which followed *Bartholomew Fair* in the next year (1616), there is a capital young gallant who misbehaves at the theatre and borrows money in time of stress. Pug, the devil's imp, who is enjoying a holiday on earth, discovers during the play that hell is not so difficult as a lady of fashion.

---

[1] *Ibid.,* V, ii, p. 391.
[2] *Bartholomew Fair*, I, i, p. 156.

But in general, Jonson's pictures of Court life grow more stereotyped and further from the actual Court in intimacy of feeling. Perhaps as he grew older he felt more confident that gentility did prevail and that the frivolity which had struck him so forcibly at first was really not far-reaching in its effect.

CHAPTER II

Jonson's View of the Contemporary Stage

O man of his time was more devoted to the stage than Ben Jonson, more sensitive to its glamour, more conscious of its romantic influence upon the public, more able to realize that in the perspective of time the plays that he and his contemporaries were writing would be reckoned one of the great gifts to the world. His reflective turn of mind and his knowledge of the past enabled him to take a detached view of this tremendous fashion of play-making and play-going, to estimate its future effect, to appraise it in the light of dramatic history, to love it as the product of his own time and to lend what skill he had to the realization of its great possibilities. Consequently his plays are full of his views of the contemporary stage. He reckoned with the audience, and its influence upon the plays that were made for its consumption; he took a vital interest in how his fellows regarded their profession and what they were making of it. To gather from his text the scattered expressions upon these matters and to reconstruct from them, as far as may be, his outlook upon the contemporary stage, is the purpose of this chapter.

In that time of rival companies and rival playhouses, when writing for the stage was a means of livelihood, and competition was cruelly keen, the pleasure of the audience was the first care of the playwright. In its hands rested the success or failure of the play and the author. Court patronage could do something for its favorites; but after that picturesque group of young university men came up to London, and determined to stand or fall by the popular taste, the crowds who gathered in playhouses on the Bankside or on the fringes of Finsbury or in Golding Lane, had the award in their own hands.

The way in which Jonson reckoned with this powerful element is characteristic. In his prefaces, prologues, epilogues, and outspoken choruses, throughout the lines of the plays, he is constantly showing what the theatre-going public is like, crediting it honestly with its good points and censuring its defects, in a constructive effort to improve it.

Seated in his audience we find such representative types as the curled, tobacco-smoking gallant, who attends the play merely as a matter of fashion;[1] the man from the country who only gets to London about once in five years when Parliament is in session;[2] the habitual playgoer who remembers what the stage was like in the good old days,[3] now twenty years past; the swaggering captain whose taste in plays is not overnice;[4] the gentleman who likes to see a subtle problem subtly propounded;[5] the serving man who must have horseplay;[6] and even the blue-stocking among ladies who finds fault with

---

[1] *Every Man out of his Humour*, Induction, p. 68.
[2] *Case is Altered*, II, 4, p. 531. [3] *Cynthia's Revels*, Induction, p. 147.
[4] *Poetaster*, III, 1, p. 232. [5] *Case is Altered*, I, 1, p. 518. [6] *Ibid.*

the costuming and feels consciously 'emancipated' as she calls for a stool upon the stage.[1]

Jonson's chief grievance is with those spectators, of whatever class, who lack a standard of judgment. The chief offender in this regard is the fashionable gallant. It was he who paid the largest price at the door, entered with a stir which was calculated to call attention to his costume, gave an additional sixpence for a stool and with a great flurry, seated himself upon the stage and took his tobacco in the approved fashion. His object in coming was not primarily to see the performance and let it have its way with him, but to call attention to himself by adverse criticism and jokes at the play's expense, and to enjoy the doubtful eminence of influencing the nearby auditors who were dazzled by his silk and velvet. Jonson is always picturing this unfortunate type whose momentary triumph has cost it so dear in the opinion of posterity. In perhaps his earliest extant play, *The Case is Altered*, he begins his war upon the empty conspicuousness of these 'capricious gallants' who 'will approve nothing . . . but sit dispersed, making faces and spitting, wagging their upright ears, and cry, *Filthy, Filthy* . . . to turn the good aspects of all that sit near them from what they behold.'[2] Besides wishing to call attention to their elegance, these empty-witted fashionables realise too that they must at least feign an interest in the drama. It was the thing of the moment. They desire to be thought 'of the judicious'[3] and, as is characteristic of people who deliver judgments on a subject of which they know nothing, the easiest method is to be destructive.

[1] *Staple of News*, Induction, pp. 275-276.
[2] *Case*, II, 4, pp. 531-2. [3] *Every Man out of his Humour*, Induction, p. 68.

Thus they always flout the play, if their clothes are sufficiently good to bear the scrutiny which will follow.[1] In
that pleasantly confidential Induction to *Cynthia's Revels,* where the three child-actors come out squabbling
over their little stage affairs before the play begins, one
of them acts the genteel auditor with delicate sarcasm.[2]
His genteelness covers a woeful ignorance and in a long
carping speech, he fails to make one essential point,
though he rests secure in his 'three sorts of tobacco.'
Coke who attends a puppet show in *Bartholomew Fair,*[3]
tries to act the fashionable man at the play; overpays at
the entrance, expects 'pretty, impudent boys to bring
stools, fill tobacco, fetch ale,' etc. But his manners are
too spacious for the occasion and he finds himself unable
to stand upright in the tiring-house of this toy theatre.
Fitzdottrell, the scapegoat in *The Devil is an Ass,*[4] is another of the same company. In *The New Inn* (1629), in
a confidential preface to the reader, Jonson is as virulent[5]
as when he made his first attack over thirty years before.

The reason for his vehemence is not far to seek. He
was always peculiarly sensitive to the power of prominent
people to influence society. It was this feeling which
made him so reverent toward the best phases of the Court
and so bitterly satiric when it wasted its opportunities in
wanton frivolity. The gallant whose judgment of plays
was ill-considered and who lacked the ability to make it
better-considered, afforded another example of lost opportunity. It was not his carping that Jonson minded

[1] *Every Man out of his Humour,* I, p. 73.
[2] *Cynthia's Revels,* Induction, pp. 145-6.
[3] *Bartholomew Fair,* V, 3, pp. 197-8.
[4] *Devil as an Ass,* I, 3, pp. 219-222.   [5] *New Inn,* 'To the Reader,' p. 337.

but the unfortunate prestige which his opinion had among the lesser-conditioned people in the audience: 'he is more infectious than the pestilence.'[1] In the whimsical set of articles, drawn up between author and audience in the Induction to *Bartholomew Fair*,[2] one of the chief points of the agreement is the following:

> It is also agreed, that every man here exercise his own judgment and not censure by contagion or upon trust, from another's voice or face, that sits by him, be he never so first in the commission of wit, etc.

In the early days of *Every Man out of His Humour*, when Jonson's hopes of his audience were higher, he declares that he will not spare his industry to please

> . . . attentive auditors
> Such as will join their profit with their pleasure
> And come to feed their understanding parts.[3]

He knows how he would like to have them behave in that ideal state of things of which he always had in his mind so vivid a picture. But thirty years later all that he asks is that

> they shall know a good play when they hear it: and will have the consciousness and ingenuity besides, to confess it.[4]

If over thirty years of reckoning with public audiences had shown Jonson that he must not pitch his hope of them too high, he did persist to the end in expecting an intelligent judgment of the play, not a second-hand opinion.

---

[1] *Every Man out of his Humour*, Induction, p. 68.
[2] *Bartholomew Fair*, Induction, p. 146.
[3] *Every Man out of his Humour*, Induction, p. 69.
[4] *Magnetic Lady*, Induction, p. 393.

Among the people who came to see his plays was the dull Philistine who has no mind, but accepts a set of opinions ready-made and judges most vehemently by them: 'the rude barbarous crew, a people with no brains, and yet grounded judgments; these will hiss anything that mounts above their grounded capacities.'[1] Though they are as ignorant and as carping as the gallants, Jonson does not mind them; they have not the same influence.

He was tolerant with his audience when there was anything to tolerate. With certain conservative playgoers, the old-fashioned Senecan tragedy of blood and revenge is the only favorite.[2] While he does not agree with their taste, he has a decent respect for their preference:

He that will swear *Jeronimo* or *Andronicus* are the best plays yet, shall pass unexcepted at here, as a man whose judgment shows it is constant, and hath stood still these five and twenty or thirty years. Though it be an ignorance, it is a virtuous and staid ignorance; and next to truth a confirmed error does well — such a one, the author knows where to find him.[3]

Peter Onion, groom of the hall, thinks any play a dull affair if there is not a fool in it,[4] and Gossip Tattle declares with an air of finality that her late husband thought a fool or a devil the best part of a play.[5] Jonson lets them rest happy in their preference and is well enough pleased that they have a definite predilection. He is good-naturedly amused at the theatre-goer who has a romantic leaning toward the charming young villain; he quite de-

---

[1] *Case*, II, 4, p. 531. [2] *Cynthia's Revels*, Induction, p. 147.
[3] *Bartholomew Fair*, Induction, p. 146. [4] *Case*, I, 1, p. 519.
[5] *Staple*, 1, p. 289.

lights in the ladies who scold him for checking the prodigal career of young Pennyboy:

> *Gossip Censure.* The young heir grew a fine gentleman in this last act.
> *Expectation.* So he did, Gossip, and kept the best company.
> *Mirth.* . . . . and began to be magnificent, if the churl, his father, would have let him alone.
> *Censure.* It was spitefully done of the poet, to make the chuff take him off in his height . . . [1]

In general, he finds his audience helpful and sympathetic. As Valentine says, 'The people generally are very acceptive, and apt to applaud any meritable work.'[2] He does not even despair of support from the Court; for he differentiates, as always, the substantial from the frivolous element there, and is sure of support from the more discerning part:[3]

> . . . . we mean the Court above the stairs
> And past the guard; men that have more of ears
> Than eyes to judge us . . .

Jonson felt the glamour of the life of the stage. He loved to take his audience into his confidence and share with it a glimpse of that magic land that lies behind the scenes. He shows an engaging versatility in bridging the gap between the player in his rôle and the player in his own person, teasing, cajoling, imploring the audience to like him. The Induction to *Cynthia's Revels*, conducted by three impish boy-actors, is an elaborate instance of this attitude, as is the Induction of *Bartholomew Fair* where the stage-keeper tells the audience what a thing the play was

[1] *Ibid.*, IV, I, p. 324.   [2] *Case*, II, 4, p. 531.
[3] *New Inn*, Second Epilogue, p. 384.

in the old days and the bookholder[1] comes on to make a pact with them, which is put into the correct form with the aid of a scrivener; it begins[2]

> Articles of agreement, indented between the spectators or hearers at the Hope on Bankside in the County of Surrey, on the one party and the author of *Bartholomew Fair*, in said place and county, on the other party . . .

Throughout his playwriting career, Jonson always visualised his audience as he prepared his manuscript, petted them, loved their foibles and enjoyed posing before them, bathed in the magic light of the stage. Even in *The Magnetic Lady*, in the winter of his days, he arranges a charming little introductory scene between a stage-boy and Masters Probee and Damplay who come from the fashionable element in the audience to demand a good performance. He is always letting the audience share his confidence about stage matters. If they applaud nicely after *Every Man out of His Humour*, lean Macilente will grow as fat as Sir John Falstaff.[3] Truewit, at the end of *Epicoene*, wickedly suggests that Morose, who abhors noise, may be cured if they applaud loudly enough.[4] Face, the dexterous swindler, at the end of *The Alchemist*, tries to conciliate the audience by promising that he'll spend his ill-got money on a splendid feast for them.[5]

This consciousness of his audience only increased his concern to improve its standard and to give the right direction to its powerful influence. He felt that he succeed-

---

[1] For an account of the bookholder and his duties see J. Q. Adams, *A Life of William Shakespeare*, p. 506.

[2] *Bartholomew Fair*, Induction, p. 145.

[3] *Every Man out of his Humour*, p. 159.   [4] *Epicoene*, p. 462.

[5] *Alchemist*, p. 74.

ed in some measure. In that remarkable prologue to *The Sad Shepherd*, in which he reviews his forty years' of writing for the stage, the matter of prime importance which he mentions first, is the change in the taste of his audience:[2]

> Although at first he scarce could hit the bore;
> Yet you, with patience, hearkening more and more,
> At length have grown up to him, and made known
> The working of his pen is now your own.

Whether he was as successful in improving the public's standard as he thought, one cannot say; but he accomplished a great deal by calling attention to pernicious tendencies in the drama of his time. How greatly he altered those tendencies cannot be accurately determined; but he at least made his audience conscious of the main problems of dramatic technique, raised queries in their minds, attempted a settlement, and thereby must have greatly increased the critical acumen of the average theatre-goer.

In propounding his theories of dramatic technique, he offers freely and frequently his opinion of the contemporary drama and its extraordinary development during the years that lay just behind him. He commends its good phases, points out its faults and suggests remedies, as a part of his effort to establish his own idea. In his attitude and method he is like Wordsworth who reacted strongly from the state of letters as he found it and set about correcting it, not only by his works but by formal statement of poetic theory in long and carefully com-

---

[1] On date of *Sad Shepherd*, see in Bang. *Materialien Zur Kunde Des Alteren Eng. Dram.*, W. W. Greg's preface to *Sad Shepherd*, p. 5.

[2] *Sad Shepherd*, Prologue, p. 486.

posed prefaces. It is interesting that both Jonson and
Wordsworth stand on the boundaries between centuries
and recognise in contemporary art an uncertainty of aim
which is due in part to the conflicting temper of two great
periods which meet at the century line. They both recoil
from certain unrealities of their chosen art, seek to bring
poetry nearer to life, are peculiarly sensitive to the defects
of the society of their time, and desire ardently to see
them corrected. But here the likeness ends. The things
which they were bent upon correcting and the means
which they employed, were quite different.

Enough has been written of Jonson's own theory of
comedy, how he conceived, defined and applied it in his
plays. His defense of his art is so clearly and frequently
expressed that one cannot go far astray in understanding
it. But in his outlook upon the work of his contemporaries and recent predecessors, he is often misinterpreted.
The bad temper on both sides in the 'quarrel plays' has
been exaggerated and overemphasized, with the result
that people expect personal animosity to colour all his
criticism of the contemporary stage. But if his specific
expressions of opinion are put together and judged im-
partially, they show a well-supported and constructive
criticism, thoughtful and suggestive, based upon sound
æsthetic principles. It is not too much to say, I think,
that Jonson succeeds better than any other author of the
period in conveying an adequate impression of the drama
of his time. Sidney was too early and furthermore lacked
the actual experience of playwriting; compilers like
Meres and Bolton were too categorical; pamphleteers
like Gosson were too prejudiced; later men like Suckling

in his *Sessions of the Poets,* too trivial and superficial in their point of view; Shakespeare too absorbed in the act of creating to take an objective view of his art, though that it was a subject which interested him, is evident from passages sprinkled here and there throughout his plays. But Jonson, coming to playwriting with a good knowledge of dramatic history, found a new development of playmaking with no critical tenets formulated; yet so far-reaching in its influence that it was bound to strive for a high standard of workmanship.

All his objections to the plays of the time come under the general head of lack of form, or sacrifice of form for sensational effect. Often plays seemed to be a series of loosely-strung scenes in which the sensational, the vulgar, the romantically impossible, were presented in turn, without much regard for harmony. He defines his position in the prefatory note, 'To the Reader,' attached to the 1612 quarto of the *Alchemist.*[1] Much of this preface is found in almost identical words in the *Timber,*[2] and the repetition of the same idea in different places in his work, shows how completely it possessed him. He is writing of contemporary audiences and what they like:

They commend writers as they do fencers or wrestlers, who, if they come in robustuously and put for it with a great deal of violence, are received for the braver fellows . . . . but I give thee this warning, that there is a great difference between those that, to gain the opinion of copy, utter all they can, however unfitly; and those that use election and a mean. For it is only the disease of the unskilful to think rude things greater than polished; or scattered more numerous than composed.

---

[1] *Alchemist,* 'To the Reader,' p. 3.
[2] *Timber,* ed. F. E. Schelling, 1892, p. 22. On the source of both these passages in Quintilian, see Gregory Smith, *Ben Jonson,* 1919, pp. 264-5.

Several popular types of plays give example of this lack of artistic unity; notably, the romantic comedy and the melodrama constructed on the pattern of the Senecan revenge play.

Jonson's attitude towards romantic comedy is very interesting. It was a creation of the time, perfect in Shakespeare, but in almost every other hand, showing, to some extent, unevenness of interest and uncertainty of treatment. It has defied the critics' definition from then till now. Meredith in his *Essay on Comedy*, shows what comedy is; then finding that Shakespeare's romantic comedy does not fit his definition, he gets out of the difficulty by maintaining that Shakespeare's comedy is something else.[1] Romantic comedy is indeed a hybrid and its different elements are scarcely harmonised completely by any hand but Shakespeare's. It was this hybrid quality that Jonson disliked. Phantasy and reality, physical spectacle and poetic imagery were jostled together in a way which made it impossible, save for the greatest artist, to achieve complete unity of effect.

In *Every Man out of his Humour,* Cordatus attacks a typical plot of romantic comedy for being amorphous, not an artistic entity. He says to those who commend it:[2]

You say well, but I would fain hear one of these autumn judgments define once, *Quid sit comoedia?* if he cannot, etc.

There is the point; romantic comedy cannot be precisely defined; it is of uncertain type. It allows elaborate dancing:

The concupiscence of dances and antics so reigneth as to run

---

[1] Meredith, *An Essay on Comedy*, 1897, p. 22.
[2] *Every Man out of his Humour*, III, 1, pp. 104-5.

away from nature and be afraid of her, is the only point of art that tickles the spectators.[1]

The successful author must 'beget tales, tempests and suchlike drolleries.'[2] Extravagant happenings staged with elaborate dancing, all inserted in a dramatic piece called comedy — this was something which Jonson's sense of decorum could not abide. It was more than intellectual snobbery that made him scorn to 'mix his head with other men's heels.'[3] In his masques he did just this thing and succeeded admirably. But he had no sympathy with phantasy and spectacle when it usurped the place of dramatic art. His whole objection is succinctly put in the Induction to *The Magnetic Lady*. The stage-boy explains to Master Damplay.[4]

The most of those your people call authors never dreamt of any decorum, or what was proper in the scene; but grope at it in the dark, or feel or fumble for it.

This statement explains all of Jonson's carping at the contemporary stage and the basis upon which he criticised it. He believed that there were fixed principles governing the emotions and effects proper to any literary form, and that these effects should be consciously arrived at by employing certain devices in constructing the piece. If one believed this, contemporary plays could not look finished, adequate, or clearly-handled from any point of view. While no doubt Jonson's formal criticism went too far, yet the attitude in which plays were tossed off, or carelessly reworked, or violated by superimposing stock

[1] *Alchemist*, 'To the Reader,' p. 3.
[2] *Bartholomew Fair*, Induction, p. 147.   [3] *Ibid*
[4] *Magnetic Lady*, Induction, p. 393.

scenes of ribaldry, violence or wonder, made for the very
opposite of artistic repose and completeness.

In *The Poetaster,* Captain Tucca's two pages act sample bits from stock scenes; and Jonson's selection of
these scenes is significant. They first act 'King Darius'
doleful strain':[1]

> O doleful days, O direful deadly dump
> O wicked world and worldly wickedness, etc.

The precise source of this passage has not, nor ever will be
discovered; it is Jonson's parody of a typical style of
ranting. Next comes something in 'amorous vein.' (The
way in which Tucca turns his boys systematically from
one high emotion to another, is a part of Jonson's satire).
The passage is taken from one of the few unconvincing
scenes in *The Spanish Tragedy,* where a highly pitched
love affair is precipitated, purely to meet the exigencies
of the revenge plot. Then comes 'the horrible, fierce
soldier' and the revenge-play scene where the ghost cries,
Vindicta, to the accompaniment of thunder, while someone calls murder 'in a small voice.' Next appears the
lady reviling her false suitor; and last, the high conqueror
of the Tamburlaine variety, who invokes earthquakes,
whirlwinds and hellish shades and does not forget the dismal night-raven and the tragic owl.[2] Jonson's criticism
is implied in the selection and parody of these scenes:
sensationalism of various sorts, is the chief concern. The
play exists for blood-curdling scenes or passages of rhetoric, amorous, vainglorious or mawkishly sentimental.

Is Jonson's attitude justified? When one thinks of

---

[1] *Poetaster,* III, 1, p. 232.
[2] *Poetaster,* III, 1, pp. 232-5.

Shakespeare — and fortunately or no, Shakespeare so far outdistances his contemporaries that he becomes, in casual opinion, the epitome of the drama of the time — one finds Jonson absurdly rigid and categorical, dry and unbending toward some of the most magical things in English literature. There is *A Midsummer Night's Dream* with its dancing and spectacle; Prospero and Caliban who surely ran away from nature; Richard III whose high rhetoric is only equalled by the high emotion behind it; and Hamlet's encounter with the ghost, so real a horror in the chill hour before dawn. All these are instances of the very things which Jonson condemns. But as Raleigh has shown[1] 'In nothing is Shakespeare's greatness more apparent than in his concessions to the requirements of the Elizabethan theatre, concessions made sparingly and with an ill grace by some of his contemporaries, by him offered with both hands, yet transmuted in the giving, so that what might have been a mere connivance in baseness becomes a miracle of expressive art. The audience asked for bloodshed and he gave them *Hamlet,* they asked for foolery and he gave them *King Lear.*'

But aside from Shakespeare, Jonson's criticism of the contemporary drama was, in the main, well placed. Only about ten years before he began his series of humour plays, *Tamburlaine* had appeared and had made plays of the conqueror type fashionable. The alchemy of Marlowe's verse has softened our sharper judgment of *Tamburlaine* as a dramatic structure; but it is safe to say that to his audience, the swaggering, the grotesque cruelty, all the things that one now likes least in the play, were a chief

[1] *Shakespeare*, Walter Raleigh, 1918, p. 27.

part of their enjoyment. It is only fair to remember that the same Edward Alleyn who acted in the rôle of Marlowe's great hero, derived much of his income from an interest in the bear-baiting house[1] at Paris Garden and that upon one occasion, at least, he personally supervised the baiting of a lion before King James at the Tower. His interpretation of the part of Tamburlaine would emphasize its bizarre sensationalism as well as its profound beauty. What the imitators of *Tamburlaine* saw in the play, bears out my contention. Greene's *Alphonsus* and Peele's *Alcasar* are strangely like *Tamburlaine*, but with the lovely quality gone. Jonson parodies *Alcasar* and picks out the most ludicrously swaggering scene of all for his purpose.[2] In this play the hero is supposed to have a violent passion for Calipolis, who is a faint shadow of Zenocrate. Of course they find themselves in a desert place where the lady faints for lack of food. It is this scene which Jonson's merciless and unerring hand lights upon. Alcasar disappears for a few moments and returns with the raw meat of a lioness, which he has just killed, impaled upon the point of his sword. This he offers to the delicate and fainting heroine in a punning line of blank verse, which, considering the time and place, is not the least wonderful of his achievements:

Meat of a princess, for a princess meet.[3]

That George Peele whose delicate academic wit had created the *Arraignment of Paris* and the subtle jeu d'esprit

[1] G. F. Warner, Edward Alleyn, *D. N. B.* Also Stow's *Chronicle*.
[2] *Poetaster*, III, 1, p. 255.
[3] *Works of George Peele*, ed. A. H. Bullen, 1887. 'The Battle of Alcasar,' II, ii, p. 253.

of *The Old Wives' Tale*, should be capable of such utter disregard of taste and propriety, is almost incredible. Greene in his *Groatsworth of Wit*[1] implies that Peele was forced by necessity to write things that would sell. If this is true, it explains the absolute contradiction between his earlier and later work. If he had to write things for money, the contempt in which he held the crudities of popular taste, is evident from the slap-dash way in which he met it. Jonson seeing the tremendous popularity of sensationalism and no doubt realising, too, how it pulled men like Peele away from a sincere expression of their art, was naturally vehement in his attack.

Another popular kind of play at which Jonson aims a shaft through the performance of Tucca's pageboys, is the melodrama of the Senecan revenge type. The undisputed master of this type was Kyd. His *Spanish Tragedy* is a brilliant manipulation of material to produce certain effects. Kyd knew that the public wanted horror and bloodshed and in the most skilful way he contrives to give it them at every turn. Jonson could not deny his clever adaptation of means to that end; but he must have despised the end. If Jonson wrote the additions to the *Spanish Tragedy* in 1601-2,[2] it is significant that he inserts only passages which heighten and vivify the conception of the characters. Of highly coloured incident the play was already too full. He seems to be trying to restore the balance and to bring out the latent possibilities in Kyd's consistently distorted melodrama.

---

[1] Greene, *Groatsworth of Wit*, Sheldonian Series, Oxford, 1919, p. 71.

[2] For one view of the authorship of the Addition to *Spanish Tragedy* see M. Castelain, *Ben Jonson, L'Homme et L'Oeuvre*, 1907, Appendix B, p. 886. For another view of the question, see Gregory Smith, *Ben Jonson*, pp. 188-189.

On the whole, Jonson's criticism of contemporary plays is justified. He did not, for one moment, wish the stage to cater to a small intellectual group. He recognised it as a potent element in the lives of all classes. In his own practice, he aims to present material

> . . fit for ladies; some for lords, knights, squires;
> Some for your waiting wench and city wires,
> Some for your men and daughters of Whitefriars.[1]

He did not believe that artistic standards would limit the general appeal of a play; and the popularity of his own humour plays, which were written on a definite formula, bears him out. He knew, too, that Shakespeare's tremendous popular success was not lessened by his adherence to the great dramatic principles. But seeing how all classes were united in their fondness for the stage, he regretted that some of the playwrights, on their side, were perverting the drama and making its appeal, as he pertinently says, like that of fencers or wrestlers.

Jonson realised that the production of plays as well as their composition was a matter of importance. He had had some personal experience in play-acting[2] so that he had a practical knowledge of the problems of dramatic production. It amuses him to give a humorous exaggeration of the nervous author before a performance of his play: prompting, stamping at the bookholder, swearing

---

[1] *Epicoene*, Prologue, p. 404.

[2] On Jonson's as an actor, see Gregory Smith, *Ben Jonson*, 1919, pp. 5-6 Note also the quotations from plays in the *Poetaster*, III, 1, p. 232. The quotation within the lines is very accurate, but often the arrangement of lines is not like the original. It seems to me probable that this re-arrangement of lines and the occasional omission of a line, may very well show that Jonson is quoting from memory, an actor's memory, which carries speeches and parts of plays easily.

about the properties.[1] The unfortunate stagekeeper in the Induction to *Bartholomew Fair* confesses that: 'he has (sir reverence) kicked me three or four times about the tiring-house, I thank him, for but offering to put in with my experience.'[2] More important people behind the scenes come under the disfavour of the temperamental author; for Mirth, in *The Staple of News*, has been in the tiring-house and has there observed the great man 'rolling himself up and down in the midst of them . . . his repeating head all to pieces . . . for he hath torn the book in a poetical fury and put himself to silence in dead sack.'[3] Though he relishes exaggerating the picture, there was probably much truth in it. It was doubtless his custom to be present at the first performance; for when he wrote *The Magnetic Lady*, he notes that the author will not be there, as if it were a departure from his practice.[4] It was generally understood that performing in one of his plays was a difficult business which opened the actor to the unsparing criticism of the author. In the *Satiromastix*,[5] he is forbidden to 'sit in a gallery when your comedies and interludes have entered their actions and there make vile and bad faces at every line . . . to make players afraid to take your parts.' When Shakespeare acted[6] in *Every Man in his Humour*, he perhaps had to undergo the ardent young author's criticism of his inter-

---

[1] *Cynthia's Revels*, Induction, p. 146.

[2] *Bartholomew Fair*, Induction, pp. 143-144.

[3] *Staple of News*, Induction, p. 276. [4] *Magnetic Lady*, Induction, p. 392.

[5] *Satiromastix*, in Dekker, edit. 4 vols., 1873, Vol. I, p. 261.

[6] Percy Simpson, in 'Actors and Acting' in *Shakespeare's England*, 1916, Vol. II, says: 'the only indication that he (i.e. Shakespeare) played an important part, is given in the folio text of Jonson's *Every Man in his Humour*, 1616, where his name heads the actor list.'

pretation. How well Jonson understood the share which good acting has in making good drama, is evident in his Epigram to Edward Alleyn.[1] 'Others speak, but only thou dost act,' he says, thus differentiating the rhetorical repetition of lines from the creative interpretation of them by a great actor. In concluding the Epigram he stresses the same point:

> . . . . . Tis just that who did give
> So many poets life, by one should live.

What Jonson thought of the profession of players in general, is of interest. They have an infinite capacity for good wine and capon; they are full of jests[2] and inclined to have flamboyant manners. In so far, he gives the traditional picture which still lingers in the present day. His view of their relation to other professions is of more specific interest. It is quite true that officially Jonson's age placed a social stigma on the actor. But the notion that actors were despised comes mainly from the legal regulations regarding troupes of actors and from the way in which Puritanic pamphlets emphasized this official hostility. In a community of such devoted theatre-goers, the brilliant actor of great rôles must inevitably have been a person prominent and admired. The fact, too, that theatre-managers, following James Burbage's shrewd and fair practice,[3] made their best actors also part-managers of the company, must have given the great actors additional prestige. Thus individuals lifted themselves above the stigma of the profession, so that John Stephens in his *Essays and Characters* (1615) finds it necessary to

---

[1] *Epigrams*, LXXXIX, pp. 242-3.   [2] *Bartholomew Fair*, V, 3, p. 199.
[3] J. Q. Adams, *Shakespearean Playhouses*, 1917, p. 62.

differentiate the 'common player' and explains his clas-
sification thus: 'therefore did I prefix an Epithite of
Common, to distinguish the base and artless appendants
of our city companies,' etc.[1] It is important to bear in
mind the distinction between players like Richard Burbage or Edward Alleyn and these 'common players.'
Jonson reflects this distinction in his text. While, as he
shows, there are many on the fringes of the profession, to
whom cleanliness and a good meal are unknown,[2] there
are others who, even in Tucca's prejudiced view,[3] are
'honest, gentlemanlike scoundrels, and suspected to have
some wit as well as your poets, both at drinking and
breaking of jests, and are companions for gallants.' Beside them the mere playmaker is relatively unimportant.[4]
When Ovid Senior thinks that his son may become a
playwright, he says:[5]

What, shall I have my son a stager, now? an enghle for players?
a gull, a rook, a shotclog, to make suppers and be laughed at? Pub-
lius, I will see thee on the funeral pile first.

Clove and Orange, that ridiculous pair of would-be literary men, find their chief glory in inviting players and
making suppers.[6] Histrio, the typical actor, in the *Poetaster*, is the high-handed employer of one Demetrius, 'a
dresser of plays' and contemplates engaging Crispinus

---

[1] *Shakespeare's England,* loc. cit. pp. 240-1. See also on the status of actors,
A Life of William Shakespeare, J. Q. Adams, chapter XI, especially p. 205 seq.
[2] *Poetaster,* III, 1, p. 234.
[3] *Poetaster,* III, 1, p. 231.
[4] The unimportance of securing an authorised text of a play, and the careless-
ness about assigning plays to their right authors, is another evidence that the
acted performance was the chief thing.
[5] *Poetaster,* I, 1, p. 211.
[6] *Every Man out of his Humour,* 'Characters of the Persons,' p. 64.

in a like menial task.[1] In this disregard of the importance of playwrights, Jonson doubtless saw a bitter justification of his own ideas of them. They pandered to the demand of actor and audience, without regard for the dignity of their calling, and general opinion treated them accordingly.[2]

Before going on to consider in some detail Jonson's relation to certain members of this dubious profession of playwriting, a word should be said about his attitude toward stage-scenery. Of course it was not such an important item in theatrical representation then as it is now, but his criticism of it is all of a piece with his general criticism of the contemporary stage and has an interesting bearing on the modern controversy over the artistic value of realistic stage-setting. He seems to have felt that in play scenery as well as in play structure, the spectacular effect got in the way of the proper artistic effect. Thus in the Prologue to *Every Man in his Humour,* he finds fault with the devices of realistic stagecraft because they draw attention away from the chief matter in hand. He proposes to present a play where no

> . . . . creaking thrones come down the boys to please
> Nor nimble squib is seen to make afeard
> The gentlewoman; no rolled bullet heard
> To say, it thunders; nor tempestuous drum
> Rumbles to tell you when the storm doth come.[3]

[1] *Poetaster,* Prologue, p. 2.

[2] In the passages which I have quoted, Jonson may have had special reason to put the playwright in an undignified light, if Clove and Orange and Demetrius and Crispinus represent Marston and Dekker. But aside from these special circumstances, the average playwright was a relatively unimportant person. It is this fact which has filled modern study of Elizabethan and Jacobean drama with so many difficulties of authorship, dates of composition, etc.

[3] *Every Man in his Humour,* Prologue, p. 2.

If stage devices had been perfectly handled so as to create the illusion which they attempted to arouse, Jonson would have left them uncriticised. But when they were badly managed, they only diverted the audience's attention from the play to a minor bit of clumsy spectacle.[1]

To return to Jonson's relationship to his fellow playwrights, we know that he disagreed with the artistic principle, or rather the lack of it, in most of their work. But his estimate of their general calibre, how he appraised them in the intimacies of daily life, is of value in a general study of his view of the stage. A great deal has been written about his literary quarrel[2] with certain among them in the years immediately preceding and following the beginning of the new century. In *The Case is Altered*, *Every Man out of his Humour*, *Cynthia's Revels*, and *The Poetaster*, major and minor characters have been identified with many contemporary authors of plays. The truth of these identifications can never be settled;[3] for the basis for such a settlement has vanished with the days in which the plays were written. Even at that time, the matter

---

[1] Morose, in *Epicoene*, contemplates sitting out a play that 'were nothing but fights at sea, drums, trumpet and target' (*Epicoene*, IV, 2, p. 441). In this passage Jonson by implication criticises the artificial noises which take the place of moving dramatic content.

[2] J. Q. Adams, *A Life of Wm. Shakespeare*, p. 235, insists upon the 'bad taste' and the 'arrogant ill-natured attacks' made by Jonson in the War of the theatres; but he admits (p. 330) that the lampooning on the other side was worse still. He puts the whole episode in its proper perspective (p. 330) by showing how completely Jonson was reconciled later to Dekker and Marston and the Chamberlain's men.

[3] For instance, Gregory Smith in his *Ben Jonson*, 1919, p. 15, identifies Anaides of *Cyn. Rev.* as Marston; but J. Q. Adams in *A Life of Wm. Shakespeare*, 1923, p. 322, identifies the same character with equal surety as Dekker. For detailed study of such identifications, see J. H. Penniman, *The War of the Theatres*, 1897, and by the same author, *Poetaster and Satiromastix*, 1913. See also R. A. Small, *The Stage Quarrel*, 1899.

would have been difficult: for the nature of such an attack is to be covert, to make the characters half true and
half fictitious, to glance near to actual portraiture and
away again before the reader can be quite certain, to leave
him gasping at your boldness at one moment and by the
next, feeling uncertain that any personal application was
intended. In the case of so near a contemporary as Meredith, who is known to have used actual people as the
basis for characters in his books, the identification of his
creations with their originals is difficult; and the problem
of how far the character presents the person and at what
point fiction comes in, is unpleasantly delicate.

That Jonson's portraiture was realistic enough to
touch Marston and Dekker, is evident from the plays
which they wrote in retaliation; but the chief value of the
controversy for the present purpose, is to show how far,
in his opinion, these men met his standard for the playwright. The weakness of Marston and Dekker, from his
standpoint, is exactly what one would expect. They lack
the knowledge and skill to give their productions an artistic form. The Clove and Orange of *Every Man out of his
Humour* arouse his indignation because they merely pre-
tend to have wit and scholarship.[1] They lack seriousness
of purpose. If they represent Marston and Dekker, he
recoils from their superficiality because he realises the
misfortune of having the drama in such irresponsible and
incompetent hands. In *Cynthia's Revels*, he condemns
Anaides and Hedon, variously assigned to Marston and
Dekker, for the same fault. They have no character or
judgment of their own; but finding themselves among

[1] *Every Man out of his Humour*, III, 2, pp. 96-97.

the frivolous and superficial courtiers, they imitate them and scorn the scholar, Crites,[1] whose admission at Court depends upon credentials which they do not understand. In the *Poetaster*, which is a very outspoken and definite attack upon these two men, under the names of Demetrius and Crispinus, they are at the mercy of Jonson's cruel pen for the same reason: they write plays at command, prostitute the drama for money; are illiterate, affected poseurs, who have no real foundation for the exercise of dramatic art. The remedies which he prescribes for them at the end of the play, signify his whole point of view. Crispinus is punished for his affected, high-sounding words and is charged for remedy, to

. . . let your matter run before your words.[2]

He is to be strengthened by reading Cato, Terence, and the best Greeks, in the hope that ultimately he will have some foundation of learning, some intellectual standard, in place of ludicrous and meaningless affectation. Demetrius is past redemption; for he is bidden to wear the

Coat and cap, and henceforth think thyself
No other than they make thee.[3]

Thus the main current of Jonson's attack is directed against the superficiality of these playwrights and the only remedy lies in their acquiring some sure intellectual standard.

How they received Jonson's strictures upon their common art, how well or how ill they understood them, is shown in the chief plays by which they return the charge.

[1] *Cynthia's Revels*, III, 2, pp. 165-166 and passim.
[2] *Poetaster*, V, p. 261. [3] *Ibid*.

Histriomastix, an old play probably revised by Marston about 1599, seems to have too little personal portraiture to warrant consideration here. Also *Jack Drum's Entertainment*, probably written about 1600 and from Marston's pen, is external in its criticism. If Brabant Senior is to be identified with Jonson, the only faults which he is given are that he disparages everyone and everything but himself and his own writings, and that he cultivates people with oddities of temperament, merely for the sake of dissecting their humours in his plays.[1] By these two qualities Brabant is tagged consistently throughout the play; but there is little interpretative criticism, little which enables one to reconstruct the author's conception of the person whom he is attacking. So, too, the frank bad temper of Dekker's *Satiromastix* results in a list of sins which Jonson, under the guise of Horace, is made to commit; but there is no general criticism implicit in the enumeration of his petty flaws. Like *Jack Drum's* Brabant, the Horace of *Satiromastix*[2] makes friends with people and then satirizes their foibles. He is untouched by a sympathetic feeling for human relationships. He consorts with gallants and flatters his way into their regard. He writes for hire and when attacked for his faults, he makes no defence but promises, in a servile way, to reform. The one piece of criticism which suggests a constructive point of view toward the object of this ill-tempered abuse, is found in the Prologue. Dekker says that he has refrained from attacking Horace's 'mind's deformity, whose greatness, if his critical lynx had with as nar-

[1] *Jack Drum's Entertainment*, in R. Simpson, *School of Shakespeare*, 1878, Vol. II, I, 1, p. 146; IV, 4, p. 193, etc.
[2] *Satiromastix*, in *Dramatic Works of Thomas Dekker*, London, 1873, Vol. I.

row eyes, observed in himself, as it did little spots upon others, without all disputation, Horace would not have left Horace out of *Every Man in 's Humour.*' This hints at the cause which seems to lie behind all Jonson's actions, that he has a peculiarity in his point of view, a particular way of looking at life, which to the slapdash, unreflecting Dekker appears to be a deformity of his mind.

When one turns to Marston's *What You Will,* one finds the more careful attempt of a discerning critic to get to the cause of the peculiarities which appear in Lampatho Doria (generally identified with Jonson).[1] Marston, that versatile young Oxonion,[2] no doubt felt the superiority of Jonson's artistic standard, was too volatile to submit to its severities, was irritated by it, as in this play, but ultimately won from irritation to admiration of a master whose quality he was quick to understand.

He makes the same points of attack which appear in the other plays: Lampatho courts people and then violates the claim of friendship by satirizing them in his plays; he satirizes not on principle but out of a desire for popularity, for[3]

> This is the strain that chokes the theatres;
> That makes them crack with full-stuff'd audience.
> This is your humour only in request,
> Forsooth, to rail.

He also reforms most cringeingly when taxed with his

---

[1] J. Q. Adams, *A Life of Wm. Shakespeare,* p. 323, shows how Marston's name for Jonson, Lampatho, is taken from Jonson's own description of himself in *Cynthia's Revels.*

[2] See C. H. Herford, Introduction to Mermaid edition of *Ben Jonson's Plays,* ed. Nicholson and Herford, Vol. I. Introduction, p. xxix, for Marston.

[3] *What You Will,* in Marston's Works, ed. Bullen, 1887, Vol. I, III, 2, p. 376.

failings, and accepts money, as in the *Satiromastix*.

But in addition to repeating the petulent carpings of the other attacks, Marston suggests a reason for Lampatho's failings. It lies, he thinks, in the scholar's temperament which removes Lampatho from sympathy with the age. Stiff pedantry has alienated him from the current of contemporary life; and Quadratus, (Marston?) with a certain gentleness beneath his brusque remedy, suggests[1]

> Come then, Lamp, I'll pour fresh oil into thee;
> Apply the spirit, that it may nimbly turn
> Into the habit, fashion of the age.
>
> . . . .
>
> I'll turn thee gallant: first thou shalt have a mistress, etc.

But Lampatho finds it difficult to unbend. As he admits in a moment of confidence,[2]

> A company of odd phrenetici
> Did eat my youth; and when I crept abroad,
> Finding my numbness in this nimble age,
> I fell a-railing.

This is Marston's explanation of Lampatho's oddities. He was not equal to the sprightliness of his age. He could not become a part of it. Failing that, he stood aside and dissected its follies. Marston of course exaggerated Jonson's austerity and failed to see that his aloofness was part of a settled conviction that the writer of comedies must stand apart and distort the time's follies in order to correct them. But even if this was Jonson's conscious artistic conviction, he found it easier to act upon, because

[1] *Ibid.*, p. 395. [2] *Ibid.*, p. 364.

it was congenial to his temper. Marston's criticism touches him to the quick and Dekker was not far wrong when he suggested, in his blunt way, that all Horace's actions were the result of a definite mental cast.

Thus it follows that there is a feeling, unconsciously or consciously realized by the other playwrights, that Jonson's artistic doctrine was not quite impersonal, not merely a matter of conviction, but also in part an expression of his peculiar temperament. This feeling no doubt, considerably lessened his influence upon them, made them less heedful of his strictures.

It is interesting, I think, that during a lifetime of preoccupation with the stage, Jonson did not allow its symbolic significance, its mimicry of life which is only more transient than life itself, to find expression until one of his later plays. In *The New Inn* (1629) he uses the stage twice as a figure to express certain phases of life.[1] Shakespeare was always letting the romantic idea that life was like a stage, or vice versa, come to the fore and some of the best known passages of his plays derive their chief appeal from this notion. But though no playwright could feel more nearly the relationship of drama to life than Jonson, it was not like him to let the symbolic side of the stage as a parallel to life find expression. By the time of *The New Inn,* however, he has grown more inward and familiar with existence: he does not value it beyond its worth; he loves it more and would reform it less; his humanity is fuller, nearer to Shakespeare's. Thus he makes the host say of his inn and of the guests who come and go there,[2]

---

[1] *New Inn,* I, 1, p. 345 and II, 1, p. 350. [2] *Ibid.,* I, 1, p. 345.

.... I may imagine all the world's a play,
The state of men's affairs, all passages
Of life, to spring new scenes: come in, go out
And shift, and vanish: and if I have got
A seat to sit at ease here, in mine inn
To see the comedy, and laugh and chuck
At the variety and throng of humours

. . . .

Why will you envy me my happiness?

If he had learned earlier the virtue of sitting at ease to laugh and chuck at humours, to love them and let them pass, his influence would have been more far-reaching. In viewing his whole magnificent and unrelaxing struggle for the improvement of the English stage, one feels always at the back of it the cruel truth that he who saveth his life shall lose it.

CHAPTER III

Jonson's Idea of Scholarship and his Connection with Contemporary Scholars

HE world of scholarship which Jonson knew, was spacious and exhilarating. It was a time when a scholar like Bacon, without being ridiculous, could say in a letter to Burleigh[1] that he took all knowledge to be his province and when Raleigh thought it possible for one man to write a history of the whole world.[2] In this book, moreover, he assumes the rôle of philosopher as well as historian and gives his reflections upon man, life and most eloquently of all upon death, as a running commentary on the history of events since the creation.

It was a time when the profession of scholarship did not debar a man from the life of action. Jonson's memory of his military exploits, the *spolia opima* of his fighting days,[3] was quite as dear to him as his literary triumphs. He says, as a matter of course, that the profes-

---

[1] *Works of Francis Bacon*, ed. J. Spedding, etc. London, 1862, Vol. VIII, p. 109, 'To the Lord Treasurer Burghley.'

[2] Raleigh, *History of the World*, with Life prefixed by Oldys, 2 Vols, 1736.

[3] *Conversations*, p. 480.

sion of writing is less important than the life of action,[1] and does not expect anyone to gainsay him. It was the general attitude and conduced to broad scholarship. The actual claims upon a man's time prevented that misplaced accuracy, that pedantry, which nowadays 'sicklies o'er' much of our scholarly effort. Aubrey says[2] that Raleigh 'studied most on his sea voyages where he carried always a trunk of books along with him and had nothing to divert him.' Evidently Aubrey had not been to sea, else he would have known that in those days voyaging was very diverting. His facts may not even be true in this particular case, but they are typical. It was a time when the reading of books was interspersed with the excitement of storms, encounters with enemy fleets, freebooting pirates, and the exploring of strange shores. Life and literature were brought into a juxtaposition which made each take colour from the other: adventure became strangely like tales in books and the reading and writing of books became an exhilarating adventure, a discovery of undreamed treasures.

Raleigh was not the only man who combined sea-going and literary pursuits. Donne probably wrote his *Storm* and *Calm* during an expedition into the Spanish parts of the Atlantic.[3] Lodge while sailing with Clarke to the Canaries in 1588 wrote the charming story of *Rosalynde: or Euphues Golden Legend*, about which he says, in a well-known passage:[4]

[1] *Epigram*, XCV, pp. 245-246.
> Although to write be lesser than to do,
> It is the next deed and a great one, too.

[2] Aubrey, *Brief Lives*, ed. Clark, 1898, Vol. II, p. 182.

[3] Gosse, *Life and Letters of John Donne*, 1899, I, p. 47.

[4] *Lodge's Rosalynde*, ed. W. W. Greg, London, 1907, p. xxvi.

. . . . to beguile the time with labour, I writ this book, rough, as hatched in the storms of the ocean, and feathered in the surges of many perilous seas . . . where every line was wet with surge and every humorous passage counterchecked with a storm . . .

Later, off Patagonia with Cavendish (circ. 1591) he wrote the *Margarite of America* amid 'such scanty fare, such causes of fear, so mighty discouragements and so many crosses.'[1]

Not only creative literature but research was very close to life. England's glorious triumph as a nation was as potent in scholarship as in literature. It aroused a full-blooded interest in the past, in the centuries and individuals who had been shaping this splendid thing for which life and death were freely given. Thus beside many general chronicles and histories of England there were studies of particular periods, like Bacon's *History of the Reign of Henry VII* and Camden's *England and Ireland during the Reign of Elizabeth*. There were investigations of special subjects like Selden's account of the progress of the English law from the earliest times[2] and his review of the civil government of Britain before the Norman Conquest.[3] When maritime affairs were so prominent, it was natural that James should ask him to investigate the laws and rights of the sea. The result of his investigation came out under the title of *Mare Inclausum* in 1636. There was an interest in early English literature too,[4] and the Eng-

---

[1] Gosse, *Seventeenth Century Studies*, London, 1883, p. 24.

[2] *Jani Anglorum Facies Altera*, 1610.

[3] *Analecton Anglo-Britanicon*, 1607.

[4] Selden edited six books of *Eadmer* from Sir Robert Cotton's copy. Cf. Sir Edward Fry in *D.N.B.* on Selden.

lish language came in for some historical scrutiny.[1] British antiquities were the subject of Camden's most famous work and there was a flourishing society for the study of English history and antiquities.[2] It was a vital and widespread curiosity, not an academic interest consciously adopted and pursued, which sent scholars to this field. The results of their study bore upon the marvellous national development which they had witnessed partly in their own time.

Even the classics were viewed as a kind of spoil to be conquered for England. In commending Chapman for his translation of the *Iliad* Jonson uses a figure of maritime conquest:[3]

> What treasures hast thou brought us! and what store
> Still, still, dost thou arrive with at our shore,
> To make thy honour and our wealth the more.

Chapman, capable of appreciating to the full his friend's massive learning, compares Jonson's contribution of classical lore in *Sejanus* to a jeweller's gift of treasures from 'richest stores and streams' and sees in Jonson's labours a parallel to the journeys of those lion-hearted voyagers:[4]

> So on the throat of the rude sea, he sets
> His vent'rous foot for his illustrious prize.

It is more than chance which leads these two scholars to commend each other's efforts in terms of sea ventures and conquests.

When study and voyaging went hand in hand, or fail-

---

[1] See Jonson's *English Grammar*, especially Book I, Chapter 4, remarks on *th.*, p. 436.

[2] J. E. Sandys, 'Education,' *Shakespeare's England*, Vol. I, p. 247.

[3] *Underwoods*, XX, p. 294.

[4] Chapman, 'On Sejanus, G. C.', *Works of Ben Jonson*, Vol. I, p. c

ing that, when the main impulse for research came out of
the high adventures of the time in which the researchers
lived, when scholars saw one another's efforts as highly
romantic exploits, it is no wonder that scholarship was
sometimes impatient of that accuracy and precision
which should be one of its chief qualities. But it made
compensation for this defect. If translations of the classics were sometimes indifferent to the details of their originals,[1] they caught in an enviable way the sweep and
feeling of a whole. How potent Chapman's *Homer* has
been almost in our own time. It inspired one of Keats's
most vivid sonnets and bore on to him some of that spacious feeling, that intoxication of discovery and conquest,
which Chapman had felt before him. Keats, perhaps unconsciously, describes his experience in terms of adventure: in reading Chapman's *Homer* he has felt,

> . . . . like stout Cortez when with eagle eye
> He gazed on the Pacific and his men
> Looked at each other with a wild surmise
> Silent upon a peak in Darien.

It was not Cortez but Balboa who discovered the Pacific
but the rush of Keats's imagination was as intolerant of
exactitudes as was that of some scholars of Elizabeth and
James. Would that a breath of this freshness might blow
through some of our modern scholarship.

But the enthusiasm which drove them into inaccuracies
sprang from a love of learning and scholarship which
made care about details, when one could stop to give it, a
pleasant duty. Jonson in the preface to *Sejanus*[2] de-

[1] Sandys, *loc. cit.*, p. 271.

[2] *Sejanus*, p. 272, 'To which it may be required, since I have quoted the page,
to name what editions I followed . . . For the rest, the chapter doth sufficiently direct, or the edition is not varied.'

scribes the editions of his sources with admirable precision. In talking to Drummond of the *History of the World,* he notes disapprovingly that 'Raleigh esteemed more of fame than conscience'[1] and a portion of the Punic Wars which he himself had written was altered by Raleigh and set in his book. In contrast to his high hand with facts, is Sir Henry Saville's accuracy which Jonson particularly commends:[2]

> But most we need his faith (and all have you)
> That dares not write things false, nor hide things true.

But while Jonson had a keen appreciation of scholarly precision, he had a strong aversion to a show of learning for its own sake. He makes Horace, in discussing Virgil's learning, distinguish neatly between pedantry and learning informed with spirit:[3]

> His learning savours not the school-like gloss
> That most consists in echoing words and terms
> And soonest wins a man an empty name;
> Nor any long or far-fetched circumstance
> Wrapped in the curious generalities of arts;
> But a direct and analytic sum
> Of all the worth and first effect of arts.

He is afraid that in quoting the sources of his classical material in *Sejanus,* he will be charged with pedantry:[4]

Lest in some nice nostril the quotations might savour affected, I do let you know that I abhor nothing more; and I have only done it to show my integrity in the story, etc.

He describes the meticulous scholars who make source-hunting an end in itself, with a very vigorous figure: their

---

[1] *Conversations,* XII, p. 480. [2] *Epigram,* XCV, pp. 245-6. [3] *Poetaster,* V, i, p. 250.
[4] *Sejanus.* p. 272.

'noses are ever like swine, spoiling and rooting up the Muses' garden.'[1] Strong language is warranted against pedantry or any perversion of those magic powers of intellect, man's

> . . . . best and understanding part
> The crown and strength of all his faculties.[2]

Sometimes the reason that Jonson and other scholars do not cite their sources precisely, is that their knowledge has become a part of them, is, indeed, their own because of the intellectual vigor with which they have recreated it. Thus Jonson's *Masque of Queens* is constructed upon a mass of abstruse learning in folklore and mythology which has become his own to such an extent that he writes without specific allusion to his various originals. He has written 'out of the fulness and memory of my former readings.'[3] When the Prince desired him to give the exact sources of his material, 'it proved a work of some difficulty to me to retrieve the particular authorities.'[4] But the care and exactitude of his scholarship made him equal to the task, as the full notes in the 1609 quarto bear witness. He had mastered his sources as carefully as the most exacting scholar could ask, and he had gone further and assimilated an imposing body of curious learning and poured it forth hot from his mind, in a delicately original shape. He had carried scholarship to its highest stage and turned it into a new creation.

This creative borrowing, this splendid energy to compass and surmount his sources, was one of Jonson's chief gifts. Many of his plays are almost a *cento* of earlier ma-

---

[1] *Sejanus*, p. 272. [2] *Cynthia's Revels*, I, i, p. 156.
[3] *Masque of Queens*, Dedic., p. 44. [4] *Ibid.*

terial and the *Discoveries* is such a triumphant metamorphosis of borrowings that it has deceived many critics. Even now that its tremendous obligations have been revealed by painstaking scholarship, it still maintains the character and importance of an original document. As Virgil comments in *The Poetaster:*[1]

> . . . . his true use of translating men,
> It still hath been a work of as much palm,
> In clearest judgments as to invent or make.

In the *Discoveries* itself, Jonson says that a poet should[2]

. . . . be able to convert the substance or riches of another poet to his own use . . . not as a creature that swallows what it takes in, crude, raw, or undigested: but that feeds with an appetite and hath a stomach to concoct, divide and turn all into nourishment . . .

While making this pronouncement, he is illustrating it, for several of the actual figures and ideas of this passage are indebted to Seneca's *Epistle to Lucilius*, xxxiv. Yet the idea is as much Jonson's as Seneca's: it stands the test of sincerity, for he acted upon it throughout his work. How thoroughly the material of the *Discoveries* became his own, is shown by the way in which he handled it: sometimes fusing several sentences into one, changing the order, transferring remarks, blending the material of different authors into a more or less coherent whole. It is an interesting testimony to the vitality of his effort that Castelain after a detailed study of the whole process comments: 'when he differs from his model one may be sure that the advantage for picturesqueness is always on his side.'[3]

---

[1] *Poetaster*, V, i, p. 258.   [2] M. Castelain, *Discoveries*, p. 125.
[3] M. Castelain, *Discoveries*, Introduction, p. xvi.

Jonson's ability to make his own the treasure of the past is, of course, characteristic of that time of splendid spoiling and conquest. T. Carew describes his borrowings in appropriate language. He is[1]

> . . . to bring the booty home
> Nor think it theft if the rich spoils so torn
> From conquered authors be as trophies worn.

Cartwright, with greater insight, sees not only the stealing, but the triumphant transformation of his thefts:[2]

> Thefts thus become just works: they and their grace
> Are wholly thine: thus doth the stamp and face
> Make that the King's that's ravished from the mine.

Thus what might have been a reproach becomes a tremendous compliment to Jonson's scholarship.

In his works, then, and in his profession of the scholar's faith, Jonson insists on the spirit of learning. There was little of the pedant in him. The application of intellect to mere ingenious problems was to him a crime. One of the chief ways in which he might have annoyed Vulcan and thus deserved to have his library burned would have been by making anagrams, acrostics and other ingenious perversions of wit.[3] Scholarship should be informed with creative light. It was a precious influence upon life. He prescribes a study of the classics as a cure for Crispinus's painful pretensions.[4] When Drummond wanted improving suggestions for his poetry, Jonson 'recommended to my reading Quintilian (who, he said, would tell me the faults of my verses as if he lived with me)'.[5] In

---

[1] 'To Ben Jonson after *The New Inn*,' p. 389.   [2] *Jonsonus Virbius*, p. 512.
[3] Execration upon Vulcan, *Underwoods*, LXII, p. 320.
[4] *Poetaster*, V, i, p. 261.   [5] *Conversations*, p. 470.

Jonson's own case it was, indeed, as if the classics lived
with him.

So profound was his faith in knowledge as a corrective of life that he looked to it as a cure for those vagaries
of a man which he called the Humours. True knowledge
is the norm from which man's humours diverge and only
in a return to that knowledge lies his salvation. So at the
centre of Jonson's philosophy the faculty of reason is en-
throned. In the Masque of *Hymen* the Humours are to
be overcome by Reason which is 'seated in the top of the
globe, as in the brain and highest part of man.'[1] Reason
remarks that

> . . . want of knowledge still begetteth jars
> When humorous earthlings will control the stars.[2]

And Probee in the Induction to *The Magnetic Lady* declares that humours, or want of knowledge, are 'the root
of all faction and schism both in Church and Common-
wealth.'[3] Knowledge and the power of reason are thus
the salvation of the world. It is an ardent and inclusive
creed. No wonder Jonson scorned any perversion of this
precious faculty, whether a pedantic show of learning for
its own sake, or a superficial assumption of culture as a
matter of fashion.

He is very accurate and very bitter in picturing the
fashionable pursuit of culture. The frivolous courtlings
scorn the scholar: 'You would not wish a thing to be better condemned of a society of gallants, than it (a retired
scholar) is,' says one of the child actors in the Induction
to *Cynthia's Revels*.[4] If one is ambitious socially one

---

[1] *Hymen.*, p. 22. [2] *Ibid.* [3] *Magnetic Lady*, Induction, p. 394. [4] *Cynthia's Revels*, Induction, p. 145.

must not linger in his company. He is in their frivolous regard, a 'book worm,' 'candlewaster,' with a lamp-oil smell about him and no money.¹ There was, however, a 'genteel scholarship,' a 'gentleman's knowledge' which was quite a different matter and very desirable. In *The Staple of News* the following conversation takes place:²

> *Almanack:* No, no great scholar: he writes like a gentleman.
> *Shunfield:* Pox o' your scholar.
> *Pennyboy Canter:* Pox o' your distinction
> As if a scholar were no gentleman.
> With these to write like a gentleman will in time
> Become all one as to write like an ass.
> These gentlemen! these rascals; I am sick
> Of indignation at them.

Yet even the gentleman must have some scraps of scholarship, and Jonson enjoys tremendously showing how they must visit the scholar's lodgings in secret to procure them. When Amorphous is instructing Asotus in the ways of fashion, he tells him he must consult a pedant:³

> *Asotus:* Yes, sir, he (the pedant) was at my lodging t'other morning. I gave him a doublet.
> *Amorphus:* Double your benevolence and give him the hose too; clothe you his body, he will help to apparel your mind.

It is a neat witticism and a pregnant suggestion of the contrast between the material standard of the courtling and the intellectual measure of the scholar.

Jonson was amused with the scholarly pretensions of several women of fashion. Saviolina in *Every Man out of his Humour* is a boring old humbug: 'all her jests are

---

¹ *Cynthia's Revels*, III, ii, pp. 165-6; IV, i, p. 172.
² *Staple of News*, IV, i, p. 319.
³ *Cynthia's Revels*, III, iii, p. 170.

of the stamp March was fifteen years ago."[1] So, too,
Lady Politic Would-be of *Volpone* is the harmless dab-
bler who pursues physics, painting, music and poetry
in turn and gets to the bottom of each subject in a single
sentence. Her garrulous call upon Volpone brings a welcome gaiety into that sombre play: especially where Volpone dubs her 'My madam with the everlasting voice'
and implores Mosca, in no uncertain language, 'For
hell's sake, rid her hence.'[2] But the affectations of the
Collegiate Ladies of *The Silent Woman* are more serious.
They live away from their husbands and entertain the
wits, supposedly out of a love of learning. But they show
real profundity of learning only in the subjects of clan-
destine meetings and cosmetics.[3] But we owe much to
their practice of the cosmetic arts; for Jonson puts his
charming rendering of the anonymous lines, Semper
Munditias, in the mouth of young Clerimont. In revul-
sion from the artificial beauty of these ladies, he cries:

> Give me a look, give me a face
> That makes simplicity a grace,
> Robes loosely flowing, hair as free.
> Such sweet neglect more taketh me
> Than all the adulteries of art.
> They strike mine eyes, but not my heart.[4]

Jonson thus finds opportunity for one more echo of a
pretty idea which runs from Catullus to Herrick.

But these would-be *savants* have no scholarly judgment as Truewit points out:[5] 'all their actions are gov-

---

[1] *Every Man out of his Humour*, III, iii, p. 110.   [2] *Volpone*, III, ii, p. 366.
[3] *Silent Woman*, i, p. 406; II, i, p. 413.
[4] *Ibid.*, I, i, p. 407. On their original, see Gregory Smith, *Ben Jonson*, p. 224.
[5] *Ibid.*, IV, i, p. 450.

erned by crude opinion without reason or cause . . .
They have a natural inclination sways them generally to
the worst, when they are left to themselves.' Yet they
serve the gayer purposes of comedy as well as those of
satire; especially where they call one another by their last
names in masculine fashion, and force the men to resort
to elaborate attire as a wile to catch their attention.[1]

Only when people prominent and influential in society
make a mockery of learning does Jonson grow abusive.
When an obvious ninny like Sir John Daw scoffs at learning, he thoroughly enjoys the fun. He allows Sir John
to pronounce most delectable folly about the classics
through a good part of one scene in *The Silent Woman:*[2]

Daw: There's Aristotle, a mere commonplace fellow; Plato, a
discourser; Thucydides and Livy, tedious and dry; Tacitus an entire knot, sometimes worth the untying, but seldom.

A question from Clerimont about the ancient poets brings
forth another round of whole-hearted abuse. Finally
Dauphine says: 'Why, who *do* you account for authors,
Sir John Daw?' The intrepid Daw is not staggered by
this question. He devises names as he goes along, high
sounding ones, too, to impress his questioner:[3]

Daw: Syntagma juri civilis; Corpus juris civilis; Corpus juris
canonis, the King of Spain's Bible.

'What was Syntagma, Sir?' queries Dauphine and Sir
John again meets the occasion triumphantly with 'A civil
lawyer, a Spaniard,' and goes on to expound more wonders. The discussion of local history by the country
clowns Clench, Medley, D'oge (Diogenes), Scriben and

---

[1] *Ibid.,* IV, ii, p. 439 and p. 449.   [2] *Ibid.,* II, ii, pp. 416-417.   [3] *Ibid.*

others, in *A Tale of a Tub*,[1] affords Jonson the same kind
of humorous enjoyment. It was only when scholarship
was threatened by the vicious affectation of fashionable
people that he became ill-natured.

Of his friendship with certain beloved members of that
fraternity of scholars who were his contemporaries, there
are many happy references in his work and theirs.
Through these passages one sees from another angle the
conception of scholarship in his time and the joy which its
devotees had in one another's company.

As early as 1603, we know from the *Conversations* that
Jonson and Camden were at Cotton's country house at
Connington. There after a distressing dream Jonson
went to Camden's chamber to tell him about it and be re-
assured. Probably he never gave up entirely the attitude
of pupil, seeking advice and comfort from that great
scholar, through whom, it is fairly certain, he was first
admitted into the pleasant and rewarding land of books.
To him he dedicated the 1616 copy of *Every Man in his
Humour*, significantly recalling in the dedication that as
the first fruits of his success, this play belonged properly
to his great instructor. His Epigram on Camden[2] is not
only touching in its reverence but selects for commendation the essential qualities of a scholar which Jonson had
no doubt first learned to know through his acquaintance
with this great man. The scholar's faith, his thorough
search, illumined by insight, are emphasized in the familiar poem. While the nature of Camden's writing did
not give him much opportunity for commenting on literature, he does, in his *Remaines*,[3] include Jonson in a list

---

[1] *Tale of a Tub*, I, ii, p. 443.   [2] *Epigrams*, IV, p. 227.
[3] *Remaines of a Greater Work*, London, 1605, p. 8.

WILLIAM CAMDEN

of ten modern authors whom the world will have cause to remember.

Jonson found many of the cleverest scholars among the members of the Inns of Court which he justly calls, 'the Noblest Nurseries of Humanity and Liberty in the Kingdom.' In dedicating the 1616 edition of *Every Man out of his Humour* to them, he recalls his 'friendship with divers in your societies, who as they were great names in learning, so they were no less examples of living.'[1] Thus scholarship and virtue, knowledge as the corrective of evil, went hand in hand in his experience as well as in his theory. Among the 'great names in learning' in this noble society, Selden's was particularly dear to him. When his *Titles of Honour* came out in 1614, Jonson wrote an Epistle for it in which he says:[2]

> . . . O how I do count
> Among my comings in, and see it mount,
> The gain of two such friendships, Heyward and
> Selden, two names that so much understand.

There was the point. Selden's name stood for all the things which were dearest to Jonson and which an uncertain, transitional age was least capable of comprehending. He notes that Selden has dedicated the work, not to some famous person, but to Heyward, his chamber fellow, who

> . . . knows to do
> It true respects: he will not only love,
> Embrace and cherish; but he can approve
> And estimate thy pains, as having wrought
> In the same mines of knowledge.

It is the joy of having a fellow-worker, someone to esti-

---

[1] *Every Man out of his Humour*, Dedic., p. 61. [2] *Epigram*, XXXI, p. 301.

mate the pains of scholarship, which bound Jonson to men like Selden and Heyward and Camden, and enabled him by their comfort to turn an arrogant front to his ignorant and superficial detractors. He and Selden shared their enthusiasms and their researches. Selden tells how lacking a copy of the scholiast on Euripides' *Orestes*, 'I went . . . to see it in the well-furnished library of my beloved friend, M. Ben. Jonson, whose special worth in literature, accurate judgment and performance, known only to that few who are truly able to know him, hath had for me ever since I began to learn, an increasing admiration.'[1] Selden undertook two pieces of investigation at Jonson's special request: one on the meaning of the Scripture forbidding the counterfeiting of sexes by apparel,[2] and one on the custom of giving crowns of laurel to poets.[3] He helped Jonson in compiling material for his History.[4] Jonson was the happy possessor of at least one author's copy of Selden: for at Sotheby's Sale of July 23, 1906, a copy of Selden's *Jani Angiorum Facies Altera* (1610) appeared, with this inscription on the title-page in Jonson's hand; 'Su Ben: Jonsonii Liber ex dono authoris mihi chariss.'[5]

In his Epistle for the *Titles of Honour*, Jonson sum-

---

[1] *Titles of Honour*, 1614, Preface, p. 6.

[2] *Joannes Seldeni, Opera Omnia*, ed. David Wilkins, 1725, Vol. II, Tom. ii, p. 1690. In *The Elizabethan Stage*, E. K. Chambers, 1923, Vol. I, p. 262, note 1, Chambers says of Jonson's request to Selden to investigate the question of sex-apparel: 'I suppose that the treatise . . was meant to furnish annotations for *B. Fair*,' i.e. as an annotation of Act V, Sc. iii. As the play was acted in 1614 and Selden's investigation was made in 1616, Chambers must think that Jonson originally intended *B. Fair* for inclusion in the 1616 edition of his *Works*.

[3] *Joannes Seldeni, Opera Omnia*, 2nd part, XLIII, p. 460.

[4] *Underwoods*, 'An Execration upon Vulcan,' p. 321.

[5] 'Books from Library of Ben Jonson,' *Trans. of Roy. Soc. of Lit. of United Kingdom*, Vol. XXVII, London, 1917, Robert W. Ramsey.

marises the qualities of Selden's scholarship: they give
an epitome of his idea of the scholar. Selden is exhaustive
and accurate in his research and uses his learning for the
correction of error:[1]

> What fables have you vexed, what truth redeemed,
> Antiquities searched, opinion disesteemed,
> Impostures branded, and authorities urged?
> What blots and errors have you watched and purged
> Records and authors of! how rectified
> Times, manners, customs! innovation spied!

In this passage Selden appears as the 'beau ideal' of meticulous scholarship: but he does not stop there. He
amasses his knowledge only to pour it forth again, to inform and teach:

> . . . . is't your wealth and will
> T'inform and teach? or your unwearied pain
> Of gathering? bounty in pouring out again?

In the light of Jonson's ideal and practice of scholarship
these verses to Selden assume more than the colour of
formal compliment; in Selden he sees his ideal person-
ified.

It is no wonder that when young Mr. Hyde (afterwards the first Lord Clarendon) came up to London to
study law in 1625 and by happy chance made the acquaintance of such men as Selden and Jonson, he decid-
ed not to let his studies have too tyrannical a hold upon
him but set apart a portion of each day to spend in such
exhilarating company.[2]

---

[1] *Underwoods*, XXI, p. 301.
[2] *Life of Clarendon*, by himself. Printed from original manuscript, Dublin, 1760, p. 7.

He always gave himself at dinner to those who used to meet together at that hour and in such places as was mutually agreed between them; where they enjoyed themselves with great delight and
public reputation for the innocence and sharpness and learning of
their conversation.

Jonson's admiration for Bacon and the influence
which Bacon had on his work,[1] is another piece of evidence which ranges him on the creative rather than the
pedantic side of scholarship. In discussing style in literature, he cites the very passage where Bacon makes his
most telling attack on pedantry:[2]

It was well noted by the late L. St. Alban, that the study of words
is the first distemper of learning . . . All these are the cobwebs
of learning and to let them grow in us is either sluttish or foolish.

He particularly commends Bacon's *Novum Organum* because 'it really openeth all defects of learning.' He re-
joices to see a gigantic intellect like Bacon's taking arms
against the perils that beset scholarship.

With Selden, Camden, Bacon and others Jonson was
one of the privileged group who enjoyed Sir Robert Cotton's library, opening onto a Thameside garden in Westminster, near Old Palace Yard.[3] His librarian, Richard
James, nephew of Dr. Thomas James, first librarian of
the Bodleian, was a very scholarly young man and enjoyed a peculiar advantage in associating with so many
brilliant men. He comments on Jonson's quality of
scholarship. He says[4]

[1] Gregory Smith, *Ben Jonson*, p. 270. C. Crawford, *Collectanea*, 2nd Series,
1907, p. 104.

[2] *Discoveries*, ed. Castelain, p. 107.

[3] Sir Sidney Lee, *D. N. B.* on Sir Robert Cotton.

[4] *Iter Lancastrense*, 1636, ed. Rev. Thos. Corser, Chetham Society, 1845,
p. xlix.

> Your rich Mosaique workes, inled (sic) by art
> And curious industry with every part
> And choice of all the Ancients . . .

His use of the word 'Mosaique' is interesting; he sees Jonson's borrowings from the Classics as set in a pattern, constructed into a whole. In a Latin letter to Dr. Francis James of Christ Church, he maintains, with quotations from Catullus supported by Horace, that Jonson's art stands comparison with antiquity and is secure of future fame.[1]

Considering the large share of Jonson's activity which went into translation and the peculiarly constructive quality of his own work in that field, it is interesting to see how he appraises his contemporary translators. He was thoroughly in sympathy with Chapman's attitude; the latter's pronouncement of the ideal of the translator, in his Preface to the *Iliad* reads like Jonson's own:[2]

Always concerning how pedantical and absurd an affectation it is in the interpretation of any author . . to turn them word for word; when . . . it is the part of every knowing and judicial interpreter, not to follow the number and order of words, but the matter and sentences to weigh diligently; and to clothe and adorn them with words and such style and form of narration, as are most apt for the language into which they are converted . . .

It is this quality which Jonson praises in the translators of his day. To Clement Edmonds, on his Translation of Cæsar's Commentaries, he writes:[3]

> Thy learned hand and true Promethean art,
> As by a new creation, part by part

. . . .

---

[1] *Iter Lancastrense*, 1636, ed. Rev. Thos. Corser, Chetham Society, 1845, p. lxx.   [2] Preface to 1611 ed. of *Iliad*.   [3] *Epigram*, CX, p. 281.

T'all future time, not only doth restore
His life but makes that he can die no more.

So, too, he commends Sir Henry Saville's Translation of
Tacitus because[1]

. . . . the soul of Tacitus
In thee, most weighty Saville, lived to us.

And Thomas May, the 'Learned Translator of Lucan'
pleases Jonson because he[2]

. . . . brought
Lucan's whole frame unto us

without the dislocation of 'the smallest joint or gentlest
word.' Owen Feltham's wicked parody of Jonson's *Ode
to Himself,* after the failure of *The New Inn,*[3] admits even
in the midst of a bad temper that he excels in the art of
translation. After Jonson's death, Feltham makes the
'amende honorable' by contributing verses to the *Jonsonus Virbius* and asks:[4]

Where shall old authors in such words be shown
As vex their ghosts that they are not their own?

It is a nice compliment, vigorously put, to the re-creative
attitude which Jonson took toward antiquity. It was this
quality which commended contemporary translators to
his hard and searching criticism.

Of Jonson's intellectual and scholarly preferences
much has been said. To dwell upon his interest in curious knowledge has not always been helpful to his reputation; for such an interest is easily taken as a sign of
pedantry. His knowledge of alchemy is supposed to be
extensive; the forthcoming edition of *The Alchemist* will

[1] *Epigram,* XCV, p. 245-6. [2] *Underwoods,* XXI, p. 294. [3] p. 386. [4] p. 514.

no doubt weigh accurately this knowledge. But the use
to which he puts his special learning in that play is so
sprightly, he subordinates his facts so competently to the
matter in hand, that his knowledge of alchemy itself is
merely by the way; it becomes a willing servant in the
house of Comedy. So, too, he shows much learning in
heraldry; but it is not an antiquarian interest for him, for
it bears directly on life.[1]

> . . . . Do not I love a herald,
> Who is the pure preserver of descents,
> The keeper fair of all nobility,
> Without which all would run into confusion?

When a knowledge of heraldry is perverted to provide
coats of arms for the 'nouveaux,' he grows indignant:

> . . . . I would tell him
> He can give arms and marks, he cannot honour;
> No more than money can make noble: it may
> Give pace and rank, but it can give no virtue.

The test of any kind of learning is that it be useful in human affairs; and the severest condemnation is that it be
perverted to improper uses.

Jonson's preference of classical to mediæval story,
while in great part, as Gregory Smith points out, the re-
action of a formalist against the insipid sweetness of the
late Spenserians,[2] is also the result of his moral judgment.
The passage in *The New Inn* which Gregory Smith cites,
shows that a large part of Jonson's objection to the stories
of old romance was moral. In this play, Lovel charac-
terizes some of the best known mediæval legends as[3]

---

[1] *Staple*, IV, i, p. 324. [2] Gregory Smith, *Ben Jonson*, pp. 286-7 and 295-6.
[3] *New Inn*, I, i, p. 349.

> Abortives of the fabulous dark cloister
> Sent out to poison Courts and infest manners.

He contrasts them with the legends of classical heroes,

> . . . . . for examples
> Of heroic virtue.

Jonson, in his own person, shows the same feeling in the *Execration upon Vulcan*. He thinks over the possible literary and scholarly enterprises which might justly annoy Vulcan to the point of burning his library:[1]

> Had I compiled from Amadis de Gaul
> The Esplandians, Arthurs, Palmerine and all,
> The learned library of Don Quixote,
> And so some goodlier monster had begot
> . . . .
> Thou then hadst had some colour for thy flames
> On such my serious follies . . .

If Jonson had known that Vulcan wanted a feast of fire, he would have offered freely

> . . . . . the whole sum
> Of errant knighthood with the dames and dwarfs
> The charmed boats and the enchanted wharfs, etc.

He would not let himself succumb to the fairyland of old romance. He makes great fun of it in *Every Man out of his Humour* where Sir Puntarvolo salutes his wife each day in the guise of a wandering knight.[2] It is but another case where he applies a rigid morality in art against his better judgment; for in talking with Drummond at Hawthornden, he ranges himself on the side of Milton, Wordsworth and Tennyson in saying that 'for an heroic

---

[1] Execration, pp. 320-321.
[2] *Every Man out of his Humour*, II, i, p. 85.

poem . . . there was no such ground as King Arthur's fiction."[1]

In summarizing Jonson's view of scholarship one is struck with the appropriateness and, at the same time, the ironic inappropriateness of the motto which he inscribed on the title-page of so many of his books, 'Tanquam Explorator.'[2] He and his contemporaries regarded scholarship as a romantic adventure: they referred to it in figures of discovery and conquest; they brought home their researches as a treasure, like the actual voyagers to strange lands. Jonson travelled as far as the bravest and brought back a golden spoil. But his passion for setting limits to limitless things, for defining qualities which ought never to be precisely defined, narrowed his view of the function of scholarship as it narrowed his view of the function of the stage.

[1] *Conversations*, X, p. 476.
[2] See Ramsey, 'Books from Library of Ben Jonson,' *loc. cit.*

CHAPTER IV

Jonson's View of Non-Dramatic Poetry

LTHOUGH Jonson was primarily interested in the drama, he could not be alive in those uncertain years which lay between Spenser and Milton without thinking about the state and future of English non-dramatic poetry. The consciousness of England had grown very strong: discoverers voyaged to find new lands for her; scholars toiled to bring to her the treasures of the past; and poets realised anew that they must formulate the laws and establish the practice of a national poetry.

It was much easier to create a conscious standard for non-dramatic poetry than for plays, where the taste of the public, from groundlings to gallants, was so powerful an influence that playwrights again and again sacrificed their artistic tenets to popular applause. But other forms of poetry, which were often circulated in manuscript for some time before their publication, reached a smaller group. While it was pleasant for the poet to have the approval of his readers, he was not absolutely dependent upon it. He could afford to become a conscious artist, following or altering an existing fashion, or evolving a new one.

There were two main sources from which he could expect guidance: the great body of classical literature, more especially Latin, in which he could see both theory and practice formulated and completed; and the still experimental attempts of Italy and France to translate new phases of a modern world into poetry. This modern literature was still evolving, poets were more interested in creating than in analysing their creations. Consequently when a critic wished to formulate the principles of poetic art, he turned away from the chaotic diversity of practice which he saw before him, to the safe iteration of theories laid down in the classics, especially in Plato and Horace.

Thus Sidney, Webbe, Sir John Harrington, Campion and other writers on poetic theory, follow the Roman morality of Horace, by insisting that the function of poetry is to uplift and improve its readers. In the broadest sense they were right, but because they took their theory ready-made from another literature, instead of deducing it from their own practice, it fits awkwardly with contemporary poetry and lacks the sincerity and immediate truth of criticism based on facts. Webbe, for example, in his *Discourse on English Poetry* (1586) maintains that poetry is 'for the instruction of manners and precepts of good life:'[1] once having set this standard, his only way of commending a poet like Chaucer, for instance, is to show the high moral effect of his poetry.[2] Thus in being true to an ancient idea, the writers on poetic theory sacrificed the truth of specific criticism. One feels the same blatant inconsistency in Campion. In his *Observations in the*

---

[1] J. Haslewood, *Ancient Critical Essays,* London, 1815, Vol. II, p. 25.
[2] *Ibid.,* p. 33.

Art of English Poesie (1602),[1] he says that poetry is 'raising the mind to a more high and lofty conceit.' He condemns rhyme as 'vulgar' and makes a plea for the adaptation of classical metres to English. Then one remembers his *Books of Airs* where the pretty conceits are far from moral and the melody springs from a delicate pattern of rhyme. The divergence between theory and practice is too wide to be called inconsistency. The educated gentleman knew classical theory and modern practice, but they were two distinct things, living apart in his mind and art.

Aristotle's generous theory, if rightly interpreted, would have shown them how such a principle could be reconciled with contemporary practice; but it was Plato rather than Aristotle who shared with Horace the place of critical dictator. Now Plato, curiously perverse to the point of view of his race and his own best self, insists upon the narrow moral aim of poetry. When Spenser, in the *Shepherd's Calendar*, maintains the ethical value of poetry, he is supported in his contention by Plato:

> O, what an honour is it (i.e. for a poet) to restrain
> The lust of lawless youth with good advice,[2]

says Cuddie. E. K. in a gloss on this passage, remarks:

This place seemeth to conspire with Plato who in his first book, De Legibus, saith that the first invention of poetry was of very virtuous intent.

There were two outstanding poets of the time who avoided the conflict between theory and practice, Jonson and Daniel. They each formulated a theory, though Jon-

---

[1] *Ibid.*, p. 162.
[2] Spenser, *Works*, ed. R. Morris, 1910, p. 477.

son's was unfortunately burned, and adhered to it in their practice. The fact that their theories were diametrically opposed, seems to me to explain the bitter animosity between them more soundly than the uncertain hypothesis of personal or professional jealousy. Jonson, of course, followed the principles laid down by classical critics, notably Horace and Quintilian, but he gave them new vitality by the very act of applying them, with some modification, to his own vigorous practice. In Jonson's work, if anywhere, the theory that poetry is to instruct, is vindicated. Daniel, on the other hand, with admirable independence of thought, did not follow the critics who professed classical theory, nor the sincere supporters of that point of view, like Ben Jonson. He says:

> Methinks we should not so soon yield our consents captive to the authority of antiquity, unless we saw more reason: all our understandings are not to be built by the square of Greece and Italy. We are the children of nature as well as they, etc.[1]

He sees the folly of attempting in English, classical metres which are based on quantity, instead of using the system of accent and rhyming which naturally belongs to the language.[2] Daniel's delicately reflective verse bears out his theory. In spite of a sonnet sequence and a good deal of Italianate verse, he felt, as he shows in the dedication to *Cleopatra*,[3] that English poetry must not be in bond to Italy any more than to Greece and Rome. In an address to English Poetry in *Musophilus*, he writes:[4]

---

[1] Haslewood, *loc. cit.*, p. 203.　[2] *Ibid.*, p. 198.

[3] *Works of Samuel Daniel*, ed. A. B. Grosart, 1885, vol. III, p. 26. Dedication to *Cleopatra*.

[4] *A Selection from the Poetry of Samuel Daniel and Michael Drayton*, Intr. by Rev. H. C. Beechy, 1899, p. 40.

Or should we (i.e. England) come behind the rest
In power of words, that go before in worth;
Wheneas our accent's equal to the best,
Is able greater wonders to bring forth?
When all that ever hotter spirits exprest
Comes bettered by the patience of the North.

This upstanding Englishman and admirably consistent artist should have commanded Jonson's respect and admiration, in an age when insincerity and superficiality were all too common in poetry; but Jonson failed to see his good qualities. He makes two of the most mincing fashionables in his plays,[1] parody portions of the *Sonnets to Delia* and the *Complaint of Rosamund*. It is interesting that Jonson selects the most artificial of Daniel's poems for parody: the elaborate figurative language of the conventional love sonnet, the conscious phrases made up of antithetical words, such as 'silent rhetoric,' 'dumb eloquence,' annoyed him. He failed to distinguish from them the sounder and more independent elements in Daniel. Furthermore, it must be admitted that Jonson had not the type of mind to appreciate the detached reflection, the slightly melancholy introspection which particularly endears Daniel to modern ears. Daniel heard the 'still, sad music of humanity' long before it became generally audible. He was astonishingly close to the early nineteenth-century romantics, in his revolt from imposed standards and in his outlook on life. His *Epistle to the Lady Margaret, Countess of Cumberland,* is like Wordsworth before his time. It is interesting that Wordsworth

[1] Matthew of *E. M. I.*, IV, i, p. 58 and Fastidious Brisk of *E. M. O.*, III, i, p. 98.

borrowed for the *Excursion*, a passage from this poem:[1]

> And that unless above himself he can
> Erect himself, how poor a thing is man.

Jonson would not fully understand this kind of wistful, subjective morality. He even missed the staunch didacticism of Daniel's *Civil Wars* and made a flippantly clever remark upon this poem in his *Conversations* with Drummond.[2]

Jonson appears badly in his judgment of Daniel, chiefly because of the divergence between their points of view. Furthermore, he had only a small residue of energy and attention for any non-dramatic poetry. His preoccupation with the stage, with the principles of dramatic structure, his evolution of a theory and practice of comedy, gave him very little time for other literary concerns. Compared with the almost inhuman consistency which characterises his dramatic work, his judgment of non-dramatic poetry is fragmentary and superficial. He had forced himself by arduous mental labour, to the creation of a new *genre* in the literature of comedy. He had thought the problem through and enunciated his conclusions. But upon non-dramatic poetry he had expended no such persistent and conscious effort. He was uncertain what its methods should be. For example, he took only a pleasantly frivolous attitude toward the burning question which had been raging since Harvey and Spenser were together at Cambridge, whether quantity or accent and rhyme were the appropriate pattern for English verse. If a similar question had come up on a matter pe-

---

[1] Excursion, IV, xi, pp. 330-331, p. 452, *Complete Poetical Works of William Wordsworth*, 1904.   [2] p. 480.

culiar to dramatic poetry, one can imagine how he would
have argued and adduced such a formidable array of precedent as would, by sheer weight, have borne down his
opponent. But his only contribution to this controversy
is a whimsical little poem written in rhyme against
rhyme, which shows an ingenious use of the art which he
is attacking:[1]

> Rhyme, the rack of finest wits,
> That expresseth but by fits
>   true conceit,
> Spoiling senses of their treasure
> Cozening judgments with a measure,
>   But false weight,
> Wresting words from their true calling
> Propping verse for fear of falling
>   To the ground, etc.

Throughout all his work, of course, Jonson is too concerned with the message of poetry, its content, to find
much time for a consideration of form. He is inclined to
regard form as the foe of meaning. In the *Conversations*
he objects to stanzas because they interrupt the flow of
thought at the wrong places.[2] He dislikes the Petrarchan
sonnet because the elaborate form distorts the meaning
to suit its pattern.[3] Though he admired Donne's poetry,
he feared that it would perish because of its obscure
meaning.[4] 'He scorned such verses as could be transposed,'[5] where the thought was so slack that it had no
definite order but followed the needs of the verse. It is
interesting that another pre-eminently intellectual figure,
Plato's Socrates, in the *Phaedrus*,[6] expresses a similar

---

[1] *Underwoods*, XLVIII, p. 311.
[2] p. 470. [3] *Ibid.*, p. 472. [4] *Ibid.*, p. 479. [5] *Ibid.*, p. 486.
[3] *Dialogues of Plato*, trans. B. Jowett, 1875, Phædrus, Vol. II, pp. 142-143.

aversion to lines that could be easily transposed. Yet
Jonson was too well trained in classical literature to de-
spise form: he regretted the lack of it in some of Donne's
verse and remarked ill-temperedly that 'Donne for not
keeping of accent deserved hanging.'[1] Drummond noticed that on the general question of the relation of form
to content, Jonson's opinions were not always consistent.
He said 'that verses stood by sense without colour or accent; which yet other times he denied.'[2] The truth of the
matter is that Jonson overstated the importance of the
material of poetry because he found too little content
and too much form in the elaborate verse of the time.
But he was too sensitive to the beauty of symmetry, to
the relationship of spirit and form, to think that either
one could live without the other.

Though he did not have time or energy for a careful
consideration of the principles and products of non-dramatic poets of his own time, he did have a clear conception of the function of poetry in general, whether in Rome
or England, regardless of the age or form in which it appeared. In fact his intellectual horizon seems wider than
that of most of his contemporaries. The generalizing
tendency of his mind, too, enabled him to see English literature merely as a phase in the evolution of world literature. In any case, he escapes the narrow patriotism of
Daniel and the distinctly contemporary fashions of verse
and thought of which Drayton's poetry is an epitome.[3]
He gets above particularities of practice and enunciates
the general principles of poetry. It is a divine gift 'not

[1] p. 471.
[2] *Ibid.*, p. 486.
[3] O. Elton, *Michael Drayton*, 1905, p. 27.

born with every man nor every day,'[1] one of the 'removed mysteries'[2] of life. It is the opposite of earthly things. The Steed of Poetry

> . . kicks at earth with a disdainful heel
> And beats at Heaven gates with her bright hoofs,[3]

But the poet is not a passive vessel into which the divine spirit comes at will. His poetry is the apotheosis of science and knowledge, the metamorphosis of intellect into something beyond understanding. It is characteristic of him to believe that the brain first must do all it can and that only when human intellect has reached its height, is it transfigured and carried into the incomprehensible realm of poetry. Thus he makes Ovid Junior describe poetry as the 'spirit of arts' and the 'soul of science.'[4] Even that most rhapsodic young person, Young Knowell, or Lorenzo Junior as he is called in the quarto of *Every Man in his Humour*, does not forget that poetry has an intellectual origin. She is[5]

> Attired in the majesty of *art*,
> Set high in *spirit*, with the precious taste
> Of sweet philosophy.

In the autobiographic Epilogue to *The New Inn* when Jonson felt his powers failing, he rejoiced that his brain was still unhurt:[6]

> . . . All strength must yield:
> Yet *judgment* would the last be in the field
> With a true poet.

In his blunt way, he pays as high a tribute to intellect, as

[1] Ded of *Queens*, p. 44. [2] *Hymen*, p. 19. [3] *Poetaster*, I, i, p. 215.
[4] *Ibid.*, I, i, p. 215. [5] Note on p. 59 of Vol. I, of *Works*.
[6] *New Inn*, p. 384.

the basis of the 'removed mysteries' of spirit and feeling, as does Plato where he shows in those beautiful myths, how understanding at its highest point, passes into something superhuman and inspired.

Wordsworth, though relying less upon the material of intellect which is accumulated in books, had the same idea when he spoke of 'steady moods of thoughtfulness Matured to inspiration.'[1]

Jonson always insists upon the moral effect of poetry; but the morality of an art which has so much inspiration in it, cannot be narrowly didactic and ethical. He agrees with Horace and Strabo about the function of the poet and translates from them in the dedication of *Volpone:*[2]

He that is said to be able to inform young men to all good disciplines, inflame grown men to all great virtues, keep old men in their best and supreme state, or, as they decline to childhood, recover them to their first strength; that comes forth the interpreter and arbiter of nature, a teacher of things divine no less than human, a master in manners; and can alone or with a few, effect the business of mankind, etc.

But when Jonson writes without any precedent in mind, about the morality of poetry, he gives it an inspiring quality which far transcends didacticism. In *The Poetaster,* he makes Tibullus say of Vergil's poetry, that it is[3]

> . . . distilled
> Through all the needful uses of our lives,
> That could a man remember but his lines,
> He could not touch at any serious point
> But he might breath his spirit out of him.

---

[1] *Complete Poetical Works of Wm. Wordsworth,* 1904, Prelude, Bk. III, pp. 148-50, p. 140.

[2] p. 333.

[3] *Poetaster,* V, i, p. 250.

Cæsar, speaking of the moral effect of poetry on the state, says:[1]

> She can so mould Rome and her monuments
> Within the liquid marble of her lines,
> That they shall stand fresh and miraculous.
>
> . . . .
>
> In her sweet streams shall our brave Roman spirits
> Chase and swim after death . . .
> . . . . . . the ambitious line
> Of the round world shall to her centre shrink,
> To hear their music.

The lover of poetry who denies to it any ulterior purpose, could not take offence at the warmth and spacious concepts of these lines.

In summary, one might say that while Jonson could only proceed by intellectual processes in the practice of poetry and while he must see for it a definite moral aim, both intellect and morality transcended their limits, were transmuted in the fires of his own burning conception of the divinity of his art. Drummond said that Jonson was[2] 'oppressed with fantasy which hath ever mastered his reason, a general disease in many poets.' While this statement fits ill with the received opinion of him, careful study shows that Drummond was not far wrong.

In the light of this view of poetry, the fashions and practices of the non-dramatic poets of his time did not assume much importance. They did not reach such a stimulating public as greeted the dramatic poetry; they felt no such keen professional competition; they did not bring their art to such close grips with reality. One goes to the *Conversations* expecting to find accurate criticism

[1] *Ibid.*, p. 248. [2] p. 494.

of them, but there is much more gossip than constructive
comment. Donne seems to have been the only non-dramatic poet who really arrested Jonson's attention. With
his poet-host, Drummond, he felt no real sympathy. He
may very well have been an agreeable guest but he seems
to have misled Drummond about his real opinion on
many points. For instance, Drummond says:[1] 'He dis-
suaded me from poetry, for that she had beggared him,
when he might have been a rich lawyer, physician or merchant.' In view of the way in which poetry lifts her arrogant head against the discomforts of poverty at several
points in his writings,[2] this statement to Drummond can
not have been sincere. He no doubt took a good deal of
whimsical pleasure in presenting himself to Drummond's
eyes as a potential 'rich lawyer, physician or merchant.'
It is equally difficult to believe that he was speaking in
good faith when he criticised Drummond's verses because
'they smelled of the schools and were not after the fashion
of the time; for a child, says he, may write after the
Greek and Latin verses in running.'[3] Surely a man who
saw how the age was too given to following fashions, too
careless of the sound tenets of these Greeks and Latins,
could not utter such a statement sincerely. In general
the opinions which Jonson expresses in the *Conversations* on contemporary poets, are very disappointing.

There was one thing which would certainly prevent
him from considering non-dramatic poetry very seriously; it was an accomplishment as well as an art, a fashionable trick of the successful courtier. He abuses roundly
the amateur versifiers at Court. In the persons of two

---

[1] p. 492.   [2] *Poetaster*, V, i, p. 249.   [3] p. 474.

precious coxcombs, Matthew of *Every Man in his Humour,* and Fastidious Brisk of *Every Man out of his Humour,* he shows what a thing a fashionable rhymer is. Matthew confesses with pride,[1]

I am melancholay myself divers times, sir, and then I do no more but take pen and paper presently, and overflow half a score or a dozen of sonnets at a sitting.

A cherished article of furniture in his study is a stool upon which to be melancholy. He courts his lady with stolen remnants of other men's verse[2] and parodies Daniel,[3] as does Fastidious Brisk in a similar situation.[4] If the fit of melancholy fails to produce verse, the courtier must.[5]

hearken out a vein and buy; provided you pay for the silence as for the work, then you may securely call it your own.

It is no wonder that Chloe, the socially ambitious citizen's wife thinks that to be a poet is a social distinction, like being a commander.[6]

Could not one get the emperor to make my husband a poet think you?

she asks with pretty ignorance.

These fashionable poetasters are of a different stripe from professional poets, and from their point of view the difference is in their favour. Sir John Daw, the prince of snobs, draws the distinction between amateur and professional verse writers:[7]

Every man that writes in verse is not a poet; you have of the wits that write verses and yet are no poets: they are poets that live by it, the poor fellows that live by it.

[1] *E. M. I.,* III, i, p. 25.   [2] *Ibid.,* IV, i, pp. 38-9.   [3] *Ibid.,* V, i, p. 58.
[4] *E. M. O.,* III, i, p. 98.   [5] *Cynthia's Revels,* III, i, p. 165.
[6] *Poetaster,* II, i, p. 220.   [7] *Silent Woman,* II, ii, p. 417.

Dauphine and Clerimont turn his point against him neatly:

> *Dauphine:* Why, would you not live by your verses, Sir John?
> *Clerimont:* No, 'twere pity he should. A knight live by his verses! he did not make them to that end, I hope.
> *Dauphine:* And yet the noble Sidney lives by his, and the noble family are not ashamed.

Jonson was not always so good humoured in his attack. He knew that such frivolous efforts brought all poetry into disrepute. Several of his characters distinguish neatly poets from poetasters: Justice Clement, Asper, Mercury and Mæcenas.[1] Speaking in his own person he puts the difference clearly in the preface to *Volpone:*[2]

> It is certain . . that the too much licence of poetasters in this time hath much deformed their mistress: that every day their manifold and manifest ignorance doth stick unnatural reproaches upon her: . . . . The writers of these days are other things, that not only their manners but their natures are inverted and nothing remaining with them of the dignity of the poet, but the abused name which every scribe usurps.

He touches with wicked accuracy another type of the enemies of poetry which is perennial: the 'hard-headed,' practical man who measures all success in terms of tangible results and by this standard, finds poetry wanting. There is a whole group of these men in the plays: the worldly, ambitious father of a dreaming, impractical son, such as Knowell Senior or Ovid Senior; successful professional and business men like Justice Overdo and Broker; and the unthinking 'man in the street' like

---

[1] *E. M. I.*, V, i, p. 58; *E. M. O.*, Induction, p. 66; *Cynthia's Revels*, II, i, p. 157; *Poetaster*, V, i, p. 248.

[2] *Volpone*, p. 333.

Tucca. They one and all discard poetry because it seems fruitless. Knowell Senior admits that he once felt the charm of the Muse:[1]

> Myself was once a student and indeed
> Fed with the selfsame humour he is now,
> Dreaming on nought but idle poetry,
> That fruitless and unprofitable art,
> Good unto none, but least to the professors.

Ovid Senior is less sympathetic. 'Are these the fruits of all my travail and expenses,' he asks. 'Name me a professed poet that his poetry did ever afford him so much as a competency.'[2] He is the pattern of the smug Philistine. The voluble and short-sighted Tucca supports him:[3] poets 'are a sort of poor starved rascals, that are ever wrapped up in foul linen; that can boast of nothing but a lean visage, peering out of a seam-rent suit, the very emblem of beggary.' From sleek Justice Overdo's point of view, poetry ruins a young man's career: 'with which idle disease if he be infected there's no hope of him in a state course.'[4] Broker confesses ruefully that Master Madrigal will not be liked by his family:[5]

> . . . . your hope
> Of Helicon will never carry here
> With our fat family: we have the dullest,
> Most unbored ears for verse . . .

Jonson handles this group with more amusement than bitterness. They are part of society in every age, irritatingly smug and short-sighted, but not so dangerous to the state of poetry as frivolous and fashionable people

---

[1] E. M. I., I, i, p. 3. [2] Poetaster, I, 1, p. 212. [3] Ibid., I, i, p. 214.
[4] Bartholomew Fair, III, i, p. 176. [5] Staple, II, i, p. 297.

who lower a great art by their inconsequential practice
of it.

Here and there throughout his work Jonson gives in-
directly his opinion of the stock conventions of this fashionable poetry. He writes wittily of the practice of com-
posing verses on articles of ladies' dress:[1]

> Such songsters there are store of; witness he
> That chanced the lace laid on a smock to see,
> And straightway spent a sonnet; with that other
> That in pure madrigal, unto his mother
> Commended the French hood and scarlet gown.

He is very amusing about himself as a possible writer of
love poetry. Jonson's sense of humour about himself is
very endearing. He saw the unfitness of his person and
mind for the light art of love. Love fled the snare of his
verses, he says.[2] In the *Celebration of Charis* he felt the
unsuitability of the lover's pose and gives a comical picture of himself as the flouted lover:[3]

> So that there I stood a stone,
> Mocked of all and called of one
> (Which with grief and wrath I heard)
> Cupid's statue with a beard;
> Or else one that played his ape,
> In a Hercules his shape.

He gives a more serious opinion of the flippant handling
of emotional and lyrical poetry in an Epigram on Bret-
on's *Melancholic Humours:*[4]

> Thou that wouldst find the habit of true passion
> And see a mind attired in perfect strains;
> Not wearing moods as gallants do a fashion,
> In these pied times, only to show their trains, etc.

[1] *Underwoods*, LXI, pp. 318-19.   [2] *Forest*, I, p. 262.
[3] *Underwoods*, p. 280.   [4] *Underwoods*, XXIII, p. 295.

Here was the heart of his criticism of the great bulk of non-dramatic verse of the time. It was the exploitation of emotions and moods for their own sakes, the 'wearing moods as gallants do a fashion.' In it, feeling was artificially conceived and expressed. The result was ingenious and pretty but not first-rate, not worth the careful consideration of a man who compounded poetry of earth and heaven and gave it the boundless realm of man's spirit to range through.

CHAPTER V

Jonson's View of the Life of the Time

LONG with the constructive criticism of social and professional groups, Jonson gives an interesting picture of daily life as he found it within doors, or abroad, in the Strand and Cheapside, at the river stairs, in the centre aisle of St. Paul's. He shows what were the diversions of leisure hours and presents the familiar face of life and custom in the various social groups which made up this great London of three centuries ago. The zest with which he observed the minutest things and the enthusiasm with which he transcribed his observations, are another evidence of his love of life. No man was further in essentials from a cynical point of view, from scorning and contemning the world in which he lived.

It is, of course, a part of his artistic economy never to bring in details for their own sake. They all serve a purpose: sometimes as a setting to interpret a character; often to extenuate a foible, by showing from what a background of superficialities it arises. Sometimes he takes a trick of fashion, like tobacco smoking, and gives different people's opinions of it, thus making it a mirror in which he shows distinctions between characters. Because he is dealing in these matters with external objects, there is no reforming tone. While he shows his sights with plenty of humour and gentle raillery, he is not bitter.

He seems actually to take one into various interiors, so accurately does he convey their atmosphere. There is Kitely's house at breakfast time.[1] The breakfast bell rings and Kitely, knowing what a dangerous thing it is to delay when a meal has been announced, sends his brother in to 'bear my wife company till I come: I'll but give orders for some dispatch of business to my servants.' Cob, the waterman, enters with his tankard, on his morning rounds, and Kitely chaffs him: 'What, Cob, our maids will have you by the back, i'faith, for coming so late this morning.' Before he has finished, Dame Kitely comes to make the petulant request, 'Sweetheart, will you come in to breakfast?' There is, too, the description of Bobadill's lodgings in Cob's house.[2] Though he plays the lavish gallant by day, he lodges humbly at the waterman's on a bench, 'with two cushions under his head and his coat wrapped about him.' When the socially aspiring young Matthew finds him there in the morning, he carries off the situation with a high hand, bids Tib set a stool for his guest and undertakes to give a lesson in duelling with two bedstaves instead of foils. The meagre upperchamber, the hard bench, the bedstaves, set off the empty pretensions of Bobadill, and at the same time show the bare neatness of the waterman's little house. Jonson gives us just a glimpse of the ample hospitality of Justice

[1] *E. M. I.*, II, i, p. 18.
[2] *Ibid.*, I, iii, pp. 11 and 12.

Clement's house in Coleman Street.[1] The kindhearted old blusterer invites his friends to supper, to celebrate the end of their difficulties. He does not forget Cob and Tib and Stephen: 'A trencher and a napkin you shall have in the buttery and keep Cob and his wife company here.' Another interesting touch suggests the nursery of Cokes Esquire of Harrow, the country boy who comes up to town for Bartholomew Fair. When he sees Nightingale selling ballads at the Fair, he says:[2] 'O sister, do you remember the ballads over the nursery chimney at home o' my pasteing up?' Albius, in *The Poetaster*, knows that interiors are an index to social position. When court society is expected to visit his humble citizen's house, he begs:[3]

. . Let not your maids set cushions in the parlour windows, nor in the dining-room windows; nor upon stools in either of them, in any case, for 'tis tavernlike . . . Hang no pictures in the hall, nor in the dining chamber, in any case, but in the gallery only, for 'tis not courtly else.

The romance of trade, already great in his day, touched Jonson's imagination. He gives two lively pictures of warehouse interiors. Kitely,[4] amid desks and keys and notes, talks of grograns and bargaining on the Exchange and bids his boy

    . . . tell over straight that Spanish gold
    And weigh it with the pieces of eight.

Albius's shrewish wife taunts him with being able only to 'marshal your pack-needles, horse combs, hobby-horses and wall candlesticks in your warehouse.'[5]

[1] *Ibid.*, V, i, p. 59. [2] *Bartholomew Fair*, III, i, p. 176.
[3] *Poetaster*, II, i, p. 218. [4] *E. M. I.*, II, i, p. 15. [5] *Poetaster*, II, i, p. 217.

Out of doors, in the London streets, there was jostle
and noise, as we know from many contemporary writers.
Jonson's text gives, with lively detail, several sources of
this hubbub. Morose, the 'gentleman that loves no
noise,' has 'been upon diverse treaties with the fish wives
and orangewomen'[1] to keep them quiet. The waits of the
city are pensioned to stay away from him; but chimney
sweepers, broommen, costermongers, brasiers, etc., will
not so easily agree to silence. He lives in a street so narrow that 'it will receive no coaches, nor carts, nor any of
these common noises.' It is the delight of his mischie-
vous nephew to tempt boisterous street entertainers into
that quiet byway:

I entreated a bearward one day to come down with the dogs of
some four parishes that way, and I thank him he did; and cried his
games under Master Morose's window . . . And another time,
a fencer marching to his prize, had his drum most tragically run
through, for taking that street in his way . . .

Amid the clatter of carriages and the cries of vendors
and the noisy crowds around street entertainers, there
was the chiming of church bells on Sundays and on holy
eves and, when thousands were dying of the plague, there
was a 'perpetuity of ringing.'[2]

If the narrow streets and the close quarters increased
the turmoil, it also brought about a delightful feeling of
accessibility and intimacy. The proximity of houses to
the streets was a disadvantage to Mrs. Otter when a
brewer's horse dashed over her crimson satin doublet and
black velvet skirts as she was taking coach;[3] but it was a
distinct advantage to the socially aspiring Sir John Daw

---

[1] *Silent Woman*, I, i, p. 408.   [2] *Silent Woman*, I, i, p. 408.
[3] *Silent Woman*, III, i, p. 425.

who 'does give plays and suppers and invites his guests
to them aloud, out of his window, as they ride by in coaches.'[1] So fully did he realise the good points of his position
that 'he has a lodging in the Strand for the purpose.'
Young Wellbred could send a note out to Young Knowell,
by a chance rider who was going in that direction. Such
a kindness was taken as a matter of course, and when the
man had delivered his letter, Old Knowell requited his
pains with the usual hospitality: 'Make this honest
friend drink here; pray you, go in.'[2] If one were giving
a dinner, at which, of course there must be music, one
could assume, in a delightfully casual way, that some
strolling band of musicians would present themselves
without special arrangement:[3]

Clerimont: The smell of venison going through the streets, will
invite the noise of fiddlers or other.
Dauphine: I would it would call the trumpeters thither.
Clerimont: Faith, there is hope: they have intelligence of all
feasts. There's good correspondence betwixt them and the London cooks: 'tis twenty to one but we have them.

All the literature of the time, of course, is full of allu-
sions to the music and singing which were everywhere in
those picturesque times. Jonson's plays are full of allu-
sions to music. A viol de gambo hung on the walls of
Madame Saviolina's court apartments and when Fastidious Brisk came thither to woo her, he took it down and
found strumming upon it a soothing accompaniment to
a difficult conversation.[4] When Deliro's wife was at odds
with him, he had only to step into the street and return
with a band of musicians to play and restore her good

[1] *Silent Woman*, I, i, p. 410.   [2] *E. M. I.*, I, i, p. 5, p. 6.
[3] *Silent Woman*, III, i, p. 426.   [4] *E. M. O.*, III, iii, p. 109.

humour.[1] Even poetry followed the pattern of music. Amorphous, the would-be courtier of *Cynthia's Revels,* composed an ode upon his lady's glove and 'set it up to my most affected instrument, the lyra.' In pointing out the excellencies of his composition, he says:[2]

> Why, do you not observe how excellently the ditty is affected in every place? that I do not marry a word of short quantity to a long note? nor an ascending syllable to a descending tone, etc.

When everybody played or sang, the performances were often tedious and a strain on one's politeness. Jonson is nowhere more delicately humorous than in the scene in Albius's house, where Hermogenes, after long urging, sings and cannot be stopped.[3] 'Nay, Hermogenes,' says Julia, hoping to stop him by her praise, 'your merit hath long since been both known and admired of us.' But Hermogenes replies, 'You shall hear me sing another.' And Julia concludes to herself: "Tis the common disease of all your musicians, that they know no mean to be entreated either to begin or end.'

At the same time that people were thronging to the theatres to see great artist productions, the narrow, crowded streets were full of catchpenny entertainments, which were almost as popular. Trained animals, especially elephants and camels and bears, were favourites and the names of their trainers were as widely known as the names of great actors and playwrights.[4] The streets were not unlike a midway in a modern county fair and poor Waspe who had the country boy, Cokes, in charge, testifies to their ruinous fascination:[5]

[1] *E. M. O.,* IV, i, p. 111.   [2] *Cynthia's Revels,* IV, i, pp. 178-9.
[3] *Poetaster,* II, i, pp. 220-222.   [4] *E. M. O.,* IV, iv, pp. 117 and 119.
[5] *Bartholomew Fair,* I, i, p. 154.

Yesterday in the afternoon, we walked London, to show the city
. . . Why, we could not meet that heathen thing all the day, but
staid him (young Cokes); he would name you all the signs over, as
he went, aloud; and where he spied a parrot or a monkey, there he
was pitched, with all the little long coats about him, male and fe-
male, no getting him away! I thought he would have run mad o'
the blackboy in Bucklersbury, that takes the scurvy, roguy tobacco
there, . . And then he is such a ravener after fruit! You will not
believe what a coil I had t'other day to compound a business between a Catherine-pear woman and him, about snatching.

The most elaborate entertainment, aside from the theatre, was the puppet-show, or 'motion.' A new motion
to be seen at Fleet-bridge, was a matter of consequence.[1]
The whole manner of presentation and the policy of the
managers is set forth in Bartholomew Fair. The performance is announced by a banner;[2] and the price of admission is on a sliding scale; 'An there come any gentlefolk,
take twopence apiece.'[3] The puppets are kept in a basket
and the showman manipulates them and talks for them
with shrewd dexterity. He confides his idea of what the
public wants:[4]

Jerusalem was a stately thing, and so was Nineveh, and the City
of Norwich, and Sodom and Gomorrah, with the rising of the prentices, and pulling down the bawdy-houses there upon Shrove Tuesday; but the Gunpowder plot, there was a get-penny . . . Your
home-born projects prove ever the best, they are so easy and familiar: they put too much learning in their things nowadays, etc.

Following his conviction, he presents a 'home-born' ver-
sion of Hero and Leander:[5]

As for the Hellespont, I imagine our Thames here: and then
Leander I make a dyer's son about Puddle wharf: and Hero a

[1] E. M. O., II, i, p. 87.   [2] Bartholomew Fair, V, i, p. 195.   [3] Ibid.
[4] Bartholomew Fair, V, i, p. 195.   [5] Ibid., V, iii, p. 199.

wench o' the Bankside, who going over one morning to Old Fish-street, Leander spies her land at Trig-stairs, etc.

While no doubt, Jonson is railing gently at the ignorance and crudity of popular taste, he probably does not exaggerate the facts. For the popularity of these motions, this may be said: in a city which had the solidarity of interest and common knowledge which is only found nowadays in a small town, the local hits and sly references to well-known abuses, which a clever showman could introduce, would give a flavour and point which would raise the entertainment above the mere manipulation of wooden puppets.

Jonson saw the colour in people even more than in objective things. He had a kinship with picturesque rascals: it was as if he realized how much he was indebted to them and returned the obligation by his genial understanding of their point of view. Thus the vendors at Bartholomew Fair are never allowed to become completely sordid, nor yet to be falsely romanticised; they are a very skilful combination of human frailties and virtues, made by an appreciative hand. Jonson was attached to the rascally beggar who poses as a disabled soldier from the foreign wars and who invents such glowing tales of his prowess as really deserve the alms he receives. Brainworm counterfeits this type of beggar. He comes forward to Ed Knowell and Stephen as they cross Moorfields, with a speech which is a triumphant combination of pride and servility:[1]

Gentlemen (he begins with a tactful word), please you change a few crowns for a very excellent good blade here? I am a poor gen-

[1] *E. M. I.*, II, ii, p. 20, p. 21.

tleman, a soldier; one that in the better state of my fortune scorned so mean a refuge, etc.

He is ready with a long account of his engagements in foreign wars, in the course of which he never fails to impress his superiority: when he served in the galleys, it was as a 'gentleman slave.' His suavity wins upon the elder Knowell in a later scene.[1] The moral old man begins by lecturing and ends by taking him into his service. No doubt Jonson had encountered many such a 'decayed, ruinous, worm-eaten gentleman of the round'[2] and loved the blatant rascality which had 'translated begging out of the old hackney pace to a fine easy amble and made it run as smooth off the tongue as a shove-groat shilling.'[3] He understood the flotsam and jetsam of humanity who struggle a little but are in general, callous of the indignities they suffer. When Puntarvolo comes to the Palace Stairs, on his way to Court, he wishes to leave his precious dog in somebody's care. A groom comes along with a basket, and the pompous, obtuse knight thrusts the dog into his hands, and gives him no reward for his pains save a long-winded injunction to 'let thy honesty be sweet as it shall be short.'[4] A basket carrier, in Puntarvolo's eyes, was *ipso facto* there to serve his wishes. The groom's reflections after Puntarvolo leaves him are well conceived: he is enraged, put upon, consumed with surly passivity. Through him Jonson glances at the sinister consequences of a lack of consideration between classes.

At this point, it is well to note that the only formal charity among the upper classes which Jonson mentions,

[1] *Ibid.*, II, iii, p. 23. [2] *Ibid.*, III, ii, p. 32. [3] *Ibid.* [4] *E. M. O.*, V, i, pp. 124-5.

is given either for social advancement or to relieve the conscience of the giver. Amorphous, when he wishes to make the acquaintance of a desirable party, thinks that he might 'talk of some hospital whose walls record his father a benefactor.'[1] Sir Epicure Mammon, when Subtle taxes him with a desire for inordinate wealth, says[2]

> I assure you
> I shall employ it in all pious uses,
> Founding of colleges and grammar schools,
> Marrying young virgins, building hospitals,
> And now and then a church.

Kitely, the merchant, is a more feeling and practical dispenser of charity. The valuable clerk in his warehouse is a foundling who had been left at his door.[3]

> I took him . . . .
> And christened him, gave him mine own name, Thomas:
> Since bred him at the Hospital . . .

Then the shrewd Kitely, seeing that the boy was capable and devoted, made him his cashier and finds

> . . . him in his place so full of faith
> That I durst trust my life into his hands.

In general, the relationship between the citizen of business and his dependents was one of the most pleasant and robust features of the time.

Jonson did not for a moment, want to break down the barriers between social groups; he merely wished the differences to be treated with respect and tolerance on both sides. Gilthead, the goldsmith, and his son, Plutarchus,

¹ *Cynthia's Revels*, I, i, p. 154.
² *Alchemist*, II, i, p. 25.
³ *E. M. I.*, II, i, p. 15.

have a long argument on being educated out of one's class. Gilthead wants his son to become a gentleman, but Plutarchus is wiser:[1]

> I do not wish to be one, truly, Father,
> In a descent or two we come to be
> Just in their (gentlemen's) state, fit to be cozened like them;
> I had rather have tarried in your trade.

In two citizen couples, Albius and Chloe of *The Poetaster*, and Otter and Mrs. Otter of *The Silent Woman*, the wives wish to get out of their class but the husbands are too well entrenched in their ways of life. Mrs. Otter provides for her husband, a retired bearbaiter, gentleman's clothes, but he will not wear them. In a fit of temper, she asks[2]

> Who gives you . . . your clean linen, your bands and cuffs, when I can get you to wear them? 'Tis mar'le you have them on now.

Cob, the waterman, enjoys picking up some fashionable foibles such as oaths[3] and the boasting of ancestry[4] . . . 'the first red herring (or Cob) that was broiled in Adam and Eve's kitchen, do I fetch my pedigree from, by the harrot's (herald's) book' . . . But on the whole he is quite content to live peaceably in his place and meet his little obligations with precise respectability:[5]

> I dwell, sir, at the sign of the Water tankard, hard by the Green Lattice: I have paid scot and lot there anytime this eighteen years.

A meek little clerk in *The Alchemist* hankers for fashionable diversions, but enjoys them very tamely and is not

---

[1] *Devil is an Ass*, III, i, p. 241.   [2] *Silent Woman*, III, i, p. 424.
[3] *E. M. I.*, I, iii, p. 12.   [4] *Ibid.*, p. 10.   [5] *Ibid.*, III, iii, p. 36.

hurt by the process. Dapper, the lawyer's clerk bets tim-idly on the races:[1]

Twice in a term or so, on Friday nights, when you had left the office, for a nag of forty or fifty shillings . . .

Drugger, the tobacco man, swaggers about being a hunt-ing gentleman, but gives himself away deliciously:[2]

In troth, we had been shooting,
And had a piece of fat ram-mutton to supper, etc.

Pheasant or venison was quite out of his experience. Su-burbia, too, imitates the fashionable world, but with no success. It merely annoys the court ladies:[3]

Phantaste: . . . This mixing in fashion, I hate it . . .
Philautia: And yet we cannot have a new peculiar court-tire but these retainers will have it; these suburb Sunday waiters; these courtiers for high days; I know not what to call them.

The foibles of society itself are the very stuff of which Jonson makes his comedies. The arbiters of fashion in-sisted upon a rigid mode of life for anyone who wished to be of their number.

Tobacco must be smoked in a prescribed way, making 'the fume come forth at's tonnels.'[4] Bobadill has used seven pounds in a week[5] and discourses volubly of differ-ent brands. Fastidious when he calls upon Saviolina at the Court finds a pipe of tobacco a social asset. He talks and puffs in the breaks of conversation and swears 'by this sweet smoke, I think your wit be all fire.'[6] Shift, 'the thread-bare shark,' has posted up in the Middle Aisle of Paul's a notice offering to teach young men 'the most gentlemanlike use of tobaccos . . . to know all

---

[1] *Alchemist*, I, i, p. 13.   [2] *Ibid.*, III, ii, p. 44.   [3] *Cynthia's Revels*, II, i, p. 163.
[4] *E. M. I.*, I, iii, p. 12.   [5] *Ibid.*, III, ii, p. 33.   [6] *E. M. O.*, III, iii, p. 109.

the delicate sweet forms for the assumption of it .
he shall receive or take in here at London and evaporate
at Uxbridge or farther, if it please him."[1] His services are
secured for Sogliardo and they hire a chamber at Horn's
ordinary for the lessons. Carlo confesses that 'I brought
some dozen or twenty gallants this morning to view them
. . . in at a keyhole, and there we might see Sogliardo
sit in a chair, holding his snout up like a sow under an
appletree, while the other opened his nostrils with a pok-
ing stick,"[2] etc. The varieties of tobacco and the elaborate devices for lighting which are found in Drugger's
shop,[3] show what a fashion smoking had become.

Kinds of food, too, were prescribed by fashion rather
than by personal taste. Carlo, speaking satirically on the
matter, tells Sogliardo that nothing is so hurtful to wit as
the eating of porridge. There is[4] 'nothing under heaven
more prejudicial to those ascending, subtle powers . . .
than your gross fare: Why, I make you an instance; your
city wives but observe them, you have not more perfect
true fools in the world bred than they are generally; and
yet you see by the fineness and delicacy of their diet (i.e.
when they are entertained by courtiers), diving into the
fat capons, drinking your rich wines, feeding off larks,
sparrows, potato pies . . . how their wits are refined
and rarefied.' The social aspirant must[5] 'learn to make
strange sauces, to eat anchovies, macaroni, bovoli, fagioli,
and caviare.' The fashionable dinner must be served in
silver dishes[6] and eaten with elaborate nicety. The dot-
ing Fallace admires the courtier's table manners:[7]

---

[1] *Ibid.*, III, i, p. 98. [2] *Ibid.*, IV, iv, p. 114. [3] *Alchemist*, I, i, p. 15.
[4] *E. M. O.*, II, i, p. 86. [5] *Cynthia's Revels*, II, i, p. 161.
[6] *Silent Woman*, III, i, p. 426. [7] IV, i, p. 111.

O fine courtier . . . . how upright he sits at the table! how daintily he carves! how sweetly he talks and tells news of this lord and of that lady! how cleanly he wipes his spoon at every spoonful of any white meat he eats! and what a neat case of toothpicks he carries about him still.

The fashionable outdoor diversions were tennis, riding, betting on races and bowling. The man of limited means had difficulty in keeping up their requirements. Hedon, of *Cynthia's Revels,* is so embarrassed for money that he can only talk about a sporting prowess which he has not experienced:[1]

He courts ladies with how many great horse he hath rid that morning . . . and sometimes ventures so far upon the virtue of his pomander, that he dares tell 'em how many shirts he has sweat at tennis that week; but wisely conceals so many dozen of balls he is on the score.

Clerimont is less hampered in his sporting tastes. He can[2]

hearken after the next horse race, or hunting-match, lay wagers, praise Puppy, or Peppercorn, Whitefoot, Franklin; swear upon Whitemane's party; speak aloud that my lords may hear you; visit my ladies at night, and be able to give them the character of every bowler or better on the green.

The ladies were occupied with suitable frivolities. They had great knowledge and skill in the use of cosmetics.[3] In the spaces between gossip and flirtations, they had their pets to occupy them. In the Palinode to Cynthia's Revels, where society folk confess their follies and ask to be absolved, there is a feeling passage on pets:[4]

[1] *Cynthia's Revels,* II, i, pp. 157-8.   [2] *Silent Woman,* I, i, p. 405.
[3] *Cynthia's Revels,* IV, i, p. 173 and V, ii, p. 191.   *Silent Woman,* I, i, p. 407.
[4] *Cynthia's Revels,* Palinode, p. 204.

Phantaste: From perfumed dogs, monkies, sparrows, dildoes and paraquettoes,
Chorus: Good Mercury defend us.

Even the books one read were often a matter of fashion. When Matthew calls upon Bobadill he has an approved volume under his arm, *The Spanish Tragedy.*[1] Fungoso, while his tailor is busy bringing his suit up to the latest fashion, will 'lie abed and read the *Arcadia* till you have done.'[2] It is a fashionable bedside book. A more sincere book lover is Dauphine of *The Silent Woman* who enjoys his bachelor retirement and reading. Truewit takes him to task:[3]

You must leave to live in your chamber, then, a month together upon Amadis de Gaul or Don Quixote . . . A wench to please a man comes not down dropping from the ceiling, as he lies on his back droning a tobacco pipe . . .

Master Probee of *The Magnetic Lady,* declares he will be content[4]

if I see a thing vively presented on the stage, that the glass of custom, which is comedy, is so held up to me by the poet, as I can therein view the daily examples of men's lives, and images of truth in their manners.

Nor can we ask for more than this. Beside the constructive criticism of life which Jonson has given in his writings, he has incidentally bestowed upon us such a gaily intimate picture of the sights and sounds and people of the great city which he loved as almost makes us dwellers in it and partakers of its charm.

[1] *E. M. I.,* I, iv, p. 13.   [2] *E. M. O.,* III, i, p. 101.
[3] *Silent Woman,* IV, i, pp. 434-435.   [4] *Magnetic Lady,* II, ii, p. 410.

CHAPTER VI

Contemporary Life as Presented by Jonson's
Fellow-Dramatists

T is an interesting fact that no writer of comedies in his day, except Ben Jonson, seemed able to produce pure comedy which reflects the social life of the time, laughs at it and stops there. That vigorous intellectual grasp which enables a man to hold the pagent of life steadily before him and see in clear, hard outlines its humours and distortions, its comical abnormalities, is a capacity of the greatest ages and of the most discriminating minds. Jonson had this ability so perfectly that perhaps the very perfection has made him unattractive and forbidding to minds of less vigor or to persons of more blended intellect and emotion. A consideration of the way in which contemporary writers of comedy make their picture of life, helps to differentiate and give one a sense of Jonson's peculiar outlook and method. A study of Chapman's comedies, for instance, at once points the difference and throws into relief the hard brilliance and austerity of Jonson's art.

When Henslowe entered in his *Diary* a 'Comedy of Umors' in 1597, referring in that phrase to Chapman's

An Humorous Day's Mirth, he was giving the typical name to one of a class of plays, of which Jonson was the most outspoken champion, but which lingered on till it became something very like itself yet very different, in the Restoration comedy of manners. There is perhaps no type of literature which reflects so subtly the difference of attitude and purpose in which it is undertaken than the study of types, ephemeral or eternal. Theophrastus, Dekker, Addison deal with the same material but throw such varying lights upon it as to make it become almost essentially different in each case.

Chapman's *An Humorous Day's Mirth*[1] preceded Jonson's first attempt at a humour play by at least a year.[2] It is very like Jonson's work and yet unlike it in the total effect. Chapman was no literary novice at the moment of undertaking it. He must have been at least thirty-seven or thirty-eight and the author of an amatory poem which was much quoted in contemporary anthologies. He had written *The Blind Beggar of Alexandria,* one of the most successful plays of the moment, if one may judge from the number of performances in the year. In this play, it had been romance and the intoxication of Renaissance possibilities, as Marlowe had put them on the stage before him, that occupied Chapman. But he also felt the newer quality of thought, arising from a detached, analytic view of life, a satiric outlook on all the concerns of mere human beings, which came with the end of the century.

[1] Printed in 1599 though mentioned in 1597 under the designation of 'A Comedy of Humours.'

[2] Tobie Mathew writing to Dudley Carleton in September, 1598, speaks of Jonson's *Every Man in his Humour,* as a new play.

To regard man's temperamental unevennesses as a result of the lack of balance in the physical elements within him, or to see human beings in terms of 'humours,' while naive and mediæval in origin, was sophisticated and subtle in the form in which it was adopted in the late sixteenth and early seventeenth centuries.[1] In *An Humorous Day'sMirth*, LeMot is an epicure in 'humours' and has a precious collection which he brings forward in the manner of a showman. There is only so much plot in the play as to display these 'humours' to best advantage, in the most characteristic postures. There are the jealous old husband, Labervele, and his pretty wife, Florilla, into whose walled-garden and close-kept Puritan thoughts, steals the lure of the wicked world; the ugly, old Countess Moren and her handsome young husband; a troupe of gallants, as indistinguishable in the play as in life, wearing correct clothes, swearing correct oaths, making correct, unoriginal remarks, which LeMot wittily foretells; and Dowsecer, the melancholy gentleman and scholar, the true satirist, who lives apart and make bitter comments on the world. A royal party is made to go and see him, to laugh at his 'humour'; but he tells them such bitter truths and sees so clearly the heart of a rotten world that they remain to admire.

There is very little action; Le Mot tastes all the 'humours' in turn and devises a meeting for them in Verone's

[1] Thus Chapman, whose long life was rich enough to embrace friendship with both Marlowe and Shirley, while he imitates the high furor of the eighties in *The Blind Beggar*, and *Bussy D'Ambois* (1607), and *The Conspiracy and Tragedy of Byron* (1608), also catches the temper of literature at the end of the century which enjoyed looking at life quizzically. So it comes about that *The Blind Beggar* and *An Humourous Day's Mirth* come near one another in time and, though they are so different, are easily accounted for by the taste of their age.

tavern under such conditions as will show each at his
height. Then he resolves their difficulties; sends Florilla
back to her garden and her Puritan thoughts; and concludes all with an impromptu mask, in which the bar-
maid, as Fortune, distributes appropriate posies of verse
for each guest.

The types, the devising of a situation to show them off,
the facile resolution of their troubles, the half-facetious
moral warning, the whole pattern, in fact, is almost exactly the one which Jonson followed in his humour plays.
The brilliant repartee of LeMot; the vacuity and foppery
of the gallants; the jealousy of old Countess Moren; the
ponderous gullibility of Labevele; the sensitive, incisive
reflections of Dowsecer, who had a little of both Jaques
and Hamlet in his temperament; all these are seen in the
light of merciless intellectual comedy and show without
blurring the weaknesses of the time. Yet Chapman cannot maintain the austerity of Jonson. His Florilla is
prettier and more gracious than such a silly young person should be; we feel more warmth for her than if she
had been created by Jonson.

Chapman, I believe, was interested in the analysis of
'humours' primarily for the sake of fun, to entertain himself in the writing and his audience in the hearing. But
Jonson sets out deliberately, knows why he presents each
person and devises each act and what result he hopes to
achieve. His earnest moral and artistic purpose shines
through from first to last, and while it makes for infinite-
ly neater workmanship, it sacrifices that spontaneity
which is the very breath of fun and good fellowship. If
one only had that lost play by Chapman, entered in the

Stationers' Register in the next year (1598) after *An Humorous Day's Mirth,* under the title, *The Fountain of New Fashions,* and could put it beside Jonson's *Cynthia's Revels* (1601) which was dedicated to 'The Special Fountain of Manners, The Court,' one would probably find a neat example of the way in which different authors' points of view transform the same material and the same pattern.

Chapman had no rigid theory about the art of comedy. Following the list of his plays chronologically, one finds that romantic comedy followed comedy of humours; then came a clever imitation of Latin comedy with some humours tucked in for good measure.[1] Then came more romantic comedy and again, in 1606, the very perfection of a humour study in *Monsieur d'Olive.* He was following rather than trying to impose the fashion, interested in all sorts of plays, not holding a brief for any one, at least so far as comedy was concerned.[2]

In *All Fools*[3] which is mainly Chapman's amalgamation of two Latin comedies, Cornelio is given the rather obvious humour, jealousy of his wife, but Chapman handles him with more indulgent good nature than Jonson shows in the treatment of Kitely in *Every Man in His*

---

[1] *All Fools* was probably written in 1599 though not printed till 1605.

[2] Only in the preface to *Cæsar and Pompey* does one find the enunciation of an artistic creed such as is so frequent in Jonson. There Chapman maintains that the only proper function of tragedy is ethical. It is probable that Chapman was as interested in the morality of art as Jonson; but, following the emphasis of classical criticism, he did not consider comedy as an artistic vehicle of the first order. If he did feel this way he was less original than Jonson who, in spite of classical precedent, believed that comedy, even more than tragedy, by reason of its frequency and popularity, must be taken up into the realm of art.

[3] Probably acted in 1599, under the title *The World Runs on Wheels,* by The Admiral's Men and revised in 1603 for performance at The Blackfriars, though not printed till 1605.

Humour. There is a pretty scene among the flowers where Cornelio tries to make pleasant conversation to his wife. Then his jealousy steals upon him and spoils the effect. But this unfortunate humour is softer, more human, pleasanter to contemplate than anything in Kitely's behavior. The play as a whole is entertaining, but it pays for its affability, as do all of Chapman's comedies, by being less of a landmark in the fast-changing history of drama than any one of Jonson's comedies.

In *Sir Giles Goosecap,*[1] the character of Sir Giles is a 'humour' *par excellence* and there is a trio of humourous gentlemen whose noses are being constantly tweaked by their witty page-boys.[2] These incorrigibles open the play with a frank discussion of their masters' foibles. It is all very like Jonson's way of describing his 'humours' before they appear. But though Sir Giles embroiders exquisitely, handles long words daringly, and courts a lady foolishly, though Foulweather is as Frenchified as possible and Rudesby a congenial third, yet the play is remembered by an entirely different group of characters. One recalls the Lady Eugenia, her uncle Momford and his scholarly friend, Clarence; the friendship of these two gentlemen and the stately courtship of Eugenia by Clarence with Momford's aid. These are the people and situ-

[1] This play was printed in 1606 anonymously but it is dated by internal evidence between 1601 and 1603 and very likely was the first play which Chapman wrote for the Children of Blackfriars. It is almost certainly Chapman's, as it parallels his thought and style in definite passages. If it was his first effort for the Blackfriars which commanded an audience of gentle and lettered people, he naturally would follow the kind of successful play recently given there, such as Jonson's *Cynthia's Revels.*

[2] Who can say that the opening dialogue between the pages is more reflective of the Italianate manner of courtiers of the day than it is imitative of those dialogues between Lyly's page-boys which were written fifteen years earlier?

ations of romantic comedy. The play is often occupied
with the analysis of emotions, or with the subtle portrayal of the romantic friendship between the two gentlemen,
or with cultivated reflections on life in general; and these
are things which stand apart from humorous knights and
witty page-boys.

Sir Giles Goosecap is a play divided against itself; it is
a hybrid made from the comedy of humours and romantic comedy. The effect is not artistic; there is no clear significance, no repose in it. It was against this hybrid
quality in both comedy and tragedy that Jonson set his
face so firmly; and, as I have shown elsewhere, in the
handling of all playwrights, save of that greatest artist, Shakespeare, this conglomerate comedy deserved his
strictures.

Monsieur d'Olive (1606) shows Chapman still uncon-
scious of any necessity to write comedy of a definite type.
The play opens with a scene of typical romantic comedy.
There is the Count St. Anne who worships his dead wife's
embalmed body, and there is a lady whose husband's
jealousy has led her to adopt a quixotic plan of life. She
lives apart and turns day into night behind closed blinds,
in a flicker of soft candle-light. But the play soon becomes the occasion for displaying a 'humour' of the Jonsonian type in Monsieur d'Olive; and with a purpose
which is Jonsonian, too.

About 1604, several embassies were sent abroad with
lavish equipment and magnificent trains of followers.
The Town was impressed with the costliness and the
glory of these undertakings. The lesser courtlings and
social aspirants mortgaged their incomes to become a

part of this greatness. Chapman found it, apparently, a disgusting affair; it was the wrong thing for governments and statesmen to sanction. As a satiric comment on the situation, he created d'Olive who appears as the head of a whimsical embassy to the King of France, to implore him to influence Count St. Anne to bury his dead lady. The scenes in which d'Olive appears to the Duke before he is given this responsible post; his report of himself as a philosopher, his weighty discussions about aristocracies and democracies and their bearing upon the use of tobacco; all these scenes display him as the prince of 'humours.'

But he is, at the same time, the satiric comment on himself and his followers. How keenly and with what bitterness he describes the pretentious rout of hangers-on who wish to join this embassy; a pawnbroker must travel with them to meet their exigencies. He understands the whole meaningless struggle of social aspirants, how they beggar their narrow resources and strive for an empty distinction. In a sparkling kind of corrective satire which suggests Jonson at his best, Chapman makes d'Olive classify the reasons why ambitious fathers send their sons abroad. Nowhere else does he turn his 'humours' to so sharp account. Yet all this is embedded in the middle of a romantic comedy and though it entirely overshadows the romantic part of the plot, it is not free of it. When Count St. Anne decides to bury his wife's body, the purpose of the embassy is gone and d'Olive wishes to retire permanently from the Court. But the courtiers have noticed his happy delusion that a certain court lady is in love with him. So they send him a letter, purporting to be from her, asking him to appear at a certain time and

in a certain disguise. He comes and they thoroughly enjoy his discomfiture. Here is humour in the modern
sense of the word, or in Shakespeare's sense, recalling to
our minds the merry predicaments of Malvolio. The bitter tone has been transformed into the fun of watching a
practical joke upon a stupid clown; and the play moves
on to show the Count and his bride in a happy ending.

Monsieur d'Olive is the very pattern of that conglomerate comedy which Jonson disliked. In this connection,
it is interesting that when modern critics commend such
a play, they cannot commend it as a whole, but for this
or that portion: the clever exposition of a romantic plot
at the opening; or the brilliant portrayal of d'Olive's
character; or the likeness of d'Olive to Malvolio in the
later acts. But nothing can be said for the comedy as an
artistic whole; Jonson's adverse criticism of this sort of
play is justified; and his effort to show in his own practice a unity of material and effect is vindicated.

I have dwelt thus at length on the handling of contemporary life and of 'humours' in Chapman's plays because,
though he was a classical scholar and understood the
ideas of categories in literature as clearly as Jonson, and
though he was willing to give the public what it wanted in
the way of amusement, he did not feel the need for holding to narrow tenets in the construction of comedies.
Though his resulting plays are entertaining, their deficiencies in unity of effect seem to show that much may be
said for Jonson's point of view.

Shakespeare does not rely upon the life of the time to
carry the entire interest of his comedies. While he allows
Hamlet to explain to the players that the function of
playing is

. . to show virtue her own feature, scorn her own image, and
the very age and body of the time his form and pressure . . .

(Hamlet III, ii)

his own artistic creed is much wider. As Polixenes explains to Perdita

> . . . . over that art
> Which you say adds to nature, is an art
> That nature makes . . . .
>
> *(The Winter's Tale* IV, iv)

Jonson would have agreed with Hamlet but he would
not have quite understood Polixenes; from his point of
view Shakespeare 'wanted art' and not even the occasion
of writing a eulogy upon his dead friend relieved him of
the embarassing necessity of making reservations about
his dramatic method. That kind of comedy which min-
gles realism and romance in a way that was abhorrent to
Jonson's neat categorical tenets, is perfectly exemplified
in *Twelfth Night.* The play opens with a line which sets
us in the midst of romantic story; a duke is in love at first
sight with a lady who is as quixotic as Count St. Anne in
her prolonged mourning for her brother. But in her
household, moving without the slightest sense of incon-
gruity among the exquisite lovers of this play, are such
types of contemporary 'humours' as Sir Andrew, Sir
Toby, and, most inimitable of all, Malvolio. A twin
brother and sister meet and recognize one another by a
stock device of Latin comedy. A fool plumbs the heights
and depths of life in moving lines, yet plays his hand with
Maria in practical jokes. There is a plot so accurately
motivated, so skillfully predestined to evolve as it does,
that the pattern of the play itself is a source of beauty;

yet all the characters in turn call upon their stars or time or chance to arrange the order of events and they call so fervently that we believe them, even while we see the artist's dexterous hand shaping all. This is the very image of conglomerate comedy which upsets all Jonson's theories, however sound they may be.

But Shakespeare's comedy almost always includes more of life than comedy calls for, even when it follows a definite pattern; *Love's Labour Lost,* for instance, overflows its bounds. *The Merry Wives,* however, which is almost purely a comedy of intrigue, a kind of dramatised Jest Book incident, is often unpopular with lovers of Shakespeare and calls upon one's memory of the Falstaff of *Henry IV* to lend it humanity and mellowness. In other words, when Shakespeare gives us comedy purely of one sort, such as Jonson would command, we are likely to have expected more and to turn away disappointed.

Dekker's picture of contemporary life in the comedies, for instance, of *Westward Ho* and *The Shoemaker's Holiday,* shows the attitude of a man as far removed as possible in temperament from Jonson. With very little to thank the world for in the way of birth and education, he yet has a hearty joy in all the simple and essential relationships of mankind, finds gentility among prentices and citizens and describes men's feelings with such deep understanding as makes his humanity, *longo intervallo,* suggest Shakespeare's. Yet sheer necessity gave him no time, and perhaps his multiform capacity for authorship gave him no inclination, to detach himself, as Jonson did, from his art long enough to see what it was all about and how he might consciously improve it.

In both *Westword Ho* and *Northward Ho,* in which he collaborated with Webster, he was occupied with the problem of the relationship of the City to the gallants. If he had been more interested in reform, as Jonson was, or had had more leisure to consider its import, he might have dealt with the question more satirically and have given the play more piquancy. But, as it stands, it is merely a fair comedy made out of the careless insolence of gallants and the awed submission of citizens' wives to their advances. Justiniano the merchant finds that his wife is likely to become a victim of an old earl's advances. He accepts the situation with admirable complacency, and for himself undertakes to frequent the City as a writing-master to citizens' wives. In the course of the action, his wife's honesty and his own rough and ready protection of her come to the fore. But in the whole play, Dekker has no crusade to make, no moral point to force home. He turns out a fairly good comedy of disguisings and intrigues, and leaves it there.

In *The Shoemaker's Holiday* he shows the stalwart way in which tradesmen hold their own even in the presence of kings, how they regard class distinctions merely as differences, without question of the inferiority of one to another. Masters and prentices recognize their obligations one to another and the whole play is full of that contentment which goes with straightforward living and the fulfillment of one's duties. But Dekker's point of view is tinged with romance; he could not resist daydreams. Pretty Rose, the shoemaker's daughter, marries a young nobleman who shows an astonishing knowledge of cobbling; and altogether the play so bursts with happy circumstance and good fortune that it leaves one with the feeling that it is almost too good to be true. In spite of the cruel pressure of a precarious existence, Dekker saw contemporary life in its rosiest colors. Some of the prettiest scenes in the play are, perhaps, as truly borrowed from life as Jonson's but they are of a very different quality. There is the scene where Ralph is being conscripted for the war, while his faithful wife, Jane, refuses to be comforted; for she is the one who stays behind. Then comes the picture of Jane in the seamster's window while Hammon outside admires her pretty hands at their work and confesses that he has stood thus many a cold winter's night to watch her bending over her sewing by candle-light. Dekker also shows us Rose in her garden, weaving garlands for Lacey and naming the flowers as she weaves.

In sum, Dekker saw life as his generous, tolerant spirit dictated, and transformed it into comedy with easy dexterity and with very little reflection upon his artistic formula. In contrast, the self-consciousness of Jonson's art becomes more clear and the grimness of his method more obvious.

After reading Middleton's comedies, one sees the justice of Jonson's idea that in order to make the depiction of contemporary life valuable, the material must be focussed and handled from some definite point of view. Middleton did not so handle his material. In *A Trick to Catch the Old One,* printed in 1607, he makes a clever play of intrigue in which a spendthrift nephew gets the better of his miserly uncle. The action goes forward against a background of London life, the noise of the tav-

ern and the people who meet there, rascally lawyers, cred-
itors and penniless courtiers. It is London life which is
not treated romantically, as it is in Dekker, nor used for
the purpose of corrective satire, as it is in Jonson. It
lacks the stability and completeness which it might have
haa, if it had been handled witht an implicit criticism of
life behind it. In *A Chaste Maid in Cheapside,* a coarse
intrigue goes on and the coarseness is only alleviated by
the presence of Tim, the son of the goldsmith, who is
home from Cambridge with his tutor and who supports
his personal dignity and the honour of his university by
speaking bad Latin on all occasions. He is a satiric comment on the academic pretentions of this City family.
He is the only bit of material which Middleton employs
for a specific purpose and consequently he is the one outstanding figure of the play.

When one turns to Marston's plays one finds in the
author a showy and shallow satirist. He was attracted by
Jonson's constructive view of life but he had too facile
and lazy a nature to endure the strictures and severities
which such a view imposed. He alternately praised and
attacked Jonson's art and made his nearest approach to
it in *The Malcontent.*

In this play, while the scene is ostensibly laid in Italy,
Marston gives us his view of the evils of court society as
it existed then in England. He is not more cruel than
Jonson toward the feebleness of the court, but he is much
less hopeful. Malevole makes those neat, satiric comments on life which Marston, no doubt, admired. Ma-
querelle, the old court bawd, jibes at the wicked intrigues
of her life; and Passerello, the court fool, touches all

things, sacred and profane, with a meditative cynicism which suggests an embittered Touchstone. The play is full of the poisonous air of a jaded court. The picture of life is not more harsh than some of Jonson's but in its implications it is more depressing. Marston chose to see no hope; he enjoyed the attitude of the brilliant cynic. It will be remembered that he had begun writing in the last years of the sixteenth century, when the fashion among the young intellectuals was satire on the model of Juvenal and Persius; and he carried this attitude to his grave, upon which, in spite of his life as a churchman, were inscribed the words: *Sacrum Oblivioni.* But Jonson, as has been shown in the chapter on his relations to the Court, had a larger vision in which the shams and pretentions of society were but a blemish on an organism which was mainly healthy, and his blacker moments are but a contrast to this greater light.

In the opening of *The Dutch Courtesan,* Marston gives a vivid picture of tavern life, where dexterous rogues mingle with fashionable young sprigs who converse affectedly. But Marston's facility and his lack of artistic seriousness allow the play soon to pass into a comedy of intrigue, following the consequences of a practical joke.

In general when Marston is cynical he is a trifle proud of it. Thus he puts us on our guard when we would appraise the value of his view of life, and when he begins a play he allows his material and whim to lead the way. In purpose and sincerity of treatment he has sacrificed the right to be considered seriously. His nonchalance has betrayed what might have been a corrective view of society, second only to Jonson's own.[1]

Heywood wrote various kinds of plays, dealing with domestic life, the affairs of the City, or romantic situations where pretty barmaids married above their station and gentlemen travelled to the far ends of the world on

[1] In 1598 in the preface to *The Scourge of Villainy* Marston has a fling at Jonson, under the name of Torquatus, for his elaborate diction and the small meaning beneath it. Probably he had already attacked Jonson, as Chrysoganus, when he retouched a dull old allegorical play, *Histriomastix*, which, though not published till 1610, was quoted by Jonson in *Every Man out of his Humour* in 1599. In 1600 (Simpson assigns the date from the fact that it was a Leap Year and the time of Kempe's Morris) he attacked Jonson again in *Jack Drum's Entertainment* which Jonson quotes in his *Poetaster* (1601). His *What You Will* (pub. 1607) was probably written soon after *Cynthia's Revels* and echoes a speech of Crites in that play. Thus Marston began his literary career with attacks upon one of the most prominent young playwrights. His antagonism to Jonson was not the result of ignorance; it was perhaps the result of bad temper. Marston was annoyed with himself for being less independent, more fond of popular favor, less able to give himself to discipline than Jonson.

Marston was not sincere: Jonson saw this defect and attacked it in *Every Man out of his Humour* and in *The Poetaster*. In *Cynthia's Revels* Jonson shows how Marston worshipped the fashionable world and affected a knowledge of languages which he did not possess.

Marston must have admitted the justice of Jonson's criticism; for in 1604 he addressed his *Malcontent* to him and paid his art a compliment in the Epilogue. He collaborated with Jonson and Chapman in *Eastward Ho* (pub. 1605). In the letters which were sent by Chapman and Jonson to the King and other influential persons asking for their release from prison where they had been put after the production of *Eastward Ho*, (see Bertram Dobell, *Athenæum*, 1901) there is no plea made for Marston; and Chapman in his letter to the King says that neither he nor Jonson wrote the objectionable passages ('two clauses and those not our own'). It is possible that Marston behaved badly in this crisis toward his two collaborators; that he loved his own popularity and safety more than the protection of his friends.

At any rate, he made another change of front; for after writing commendatory verses for Jonson's *Sejanus* in 1605, he attacked it covertly for its pedantic use of sources in the preface to *Sophonisba*, 1606. Marston however, was shrewd enough to see Jonson's defects: a rigidity and ponderosity which, in an age of sprightliness and easy adaptability, was out of place. In *What You Will* he makes Lampathio Doria, who represents Jonson, confess that after an academic life he crawls forth only to find himself too rigid for the nimble age in which he lives.

ships which always moved through blue water, under a smart breeze, with a pirate or a Spaniard lurking menacingly to leeward. The point of view which governs his characters and actions is the bourgeois conception of true gentility and noble behaviour. Thus his plays are hardly a reflection of life as it was; they are rather the reflection of the ideals of a social group which was growing in size and influence and encroaching upon the aristocratic glory of Elizabethan days. Perhaps it would not be too harsh to say that Heywood should have been a popular novelist, but that he worked in the wrong medium because it was then the most popular form of fiction.

While we may not look to his characters and their behaviour for an accurate reflection of the time, the external things of contemporary life are pleasantly shown in his plays. He presents Plymouth on the eve of Essex's great expedition to the Azores in 1597; the streets and inns are crowded with laughing gallants, going in a rollicking and high-spirited mood to face hardship and danger.[1] He shows a dark night near London Bridge, where two young maids are groping their way toward home with parcels of lawn and new ruffs when they fall unexpectedly into the clutches of two witty ruffians.[2] There are passages which by their intimate touches almost recreate the scene: in *A Woman Killed with Kindness*, Jenkins is ordered by Cicely to clean the visitors' boots and then wash his hands before serving at dinner; and in *The Gentleman Traveller*, Young Geraldine, left alone with his perplexing thoughts at midnight in a strange house, hunts about for a book to divert himself. This kind of photo-

[1] *Fair Maid of the West.*
[2] *Fair Maid of the Exchange.*

graphic accuracy in detail is pleasant; it seems to make tangible and familiar to us a remote past. But how trivial and minor an affair this sort of reflection of contemporary life is compared witth that neat, unswerving dissection of the very nerves and sinews of the time which appears in Jonson.

The comedy of Beaumont and Fletcher is interesting because of the close friendship between these two gentlemen and Jonson. In one of the earliest comedies, written probably by Beaumont alone, *The Woman-hater*, there is an effort to imitate Jonson's 'humours.' In the preface Beaumont shows what a young courtier thought of his own social group when he chose to satirize it. He maintains that a courtier may be honest or a lord wise, or that they may not be; but merely because they find their lives set in court circles they are not to be assumed to be vicious. In other words he is not prejudiced against them because they are courtiers.

His greedy Lazarillo who dares much for the sake of having a delicate fish, and Gondarino who hates women on principle, are 'humours' which consciously imitate those of Ben Jonson. But they lack the incisiveness of Jonson's exaggerations. In fact, this play only comes to life with the character of the young courtier himself, who is so bored that he goes to seek adventure, reflecting that the world is ill-arranged since the poor suffer from too much to do and the rich from too little.

This comedy, moreover, furnishes an interesting example of that artistic confusion which contrasts so strongly with the purity of Jonson's method. Toward the end, this play of 'humours' slips into romantic comedy. The beautiful Oriana, suspected by the jealous duke, her lover, has her chastity tried and prefers death to dishonour in a melodramatic scene. After this Beaumont with a tremendous effort brings the play back to end after the fashion of a comedy of humours; but the whole effect is incongruous. In this attempt to imitate Jonson, Beaumont lacks the master's breadth; he only paints to the life when his humourous young courtier becomes autobiographic.

In *The Knight of the Burning Pestle*,[1] City life is presented from a particular angle. The point of view springs from a frank realization of class differences. There is no kindness in the authors' unmerciful exposition of the City's taste in plays. Romance, from being the court literature a century or two earlier, had now become the means of feeding the cheap sentimentality of the City shopkeeper. Beaumont and Fletcher laughed at the unsophisticated citizen's wife who became so engrossed in the play that she offered a cure for the hero's chilblains and threatened to call the constable from Shoreditch when Ralph was getting the worst of it in his fight with the barber-dragon. They laughed at her not perhaps without a tinge of envy; for their own sophistication had put them beyond the pleasure of living in a play and feeling homely sympathy with its characters. Beside them Jonson seems the personification of human sympathy, for he never ridicules people merely from the point of view of social superiority.

In general, when Beaumont and Fletcher attempt Jonsonian comedy, they are not sufficiently in earnest to

---

[1] Printed anonymously, 1613.

make their comment on the foibles of the time searching, nor have they sufficient human sympathy to discover the essence of the follies they depict. Thus they fall short in pointed satire and in accurate delineation of character.

In Massinger's *A New Way to Pay Old Debts*,[1] the character of Sir Giles Overreach, the miserly uncle of a charming if prodigal nephew is drawn with a powerful and sinister touch. Massinger has a whole-hearted loathing of the vice his character possesses and his portrayal offers a fair parallel to Jonson's presentation of Volpone. The underlying idea of the play, too, that the world casts out a ragged man but honours him again when he is in good company, has in it the constructive view of corrective comedy. But a comparison with *Volpone* brings out Massinger's defects as well as his good points; for one notices in *A New Way* an absence of those minor characters like Sir Politik and Lady Would-Be, who lighten the grim satire of *Volpone* without introducing a jarring note. In place of them, Massinger, with much less skill, introduces a romantic element. The gentility and kindness of Lady Allworth and her son, while they relieve the feeling aroused by Overreach, introduce a foreign element and mar the artistic effect of the whole.

In *The City Madam*,[2] Massinger makes a sensational plot in which the effect of some Jonsonian 'humours' like Lady Frugal and Young Goldwire, is entirely lost. There is nothing constructive or gripping in the satire.

In fact, Massinger has, in isolated passages, a first-rate ability for comedy of the Jonsonian type; but he gives

[1] Published, 1633.
[2] Licensed, 1632, and printed 1658.

away his effect sometimes to romantic comedy, sometimes to melodrama.

In general, the comedies outside those of Ben Jonson,
which attempt to reproduce the life of the time, give a
much less steady and impartial view of it. Their picture
is likely to be self-conscious or restricted, or most frequently of all, colored by romance.

APPENDICES

I

References Connecting Jonson with Special Groups of Friends in the Inns of Court.

Jonson dedicates 1616 ed. of *E. M. O.* to Inns of Court with reference to his early associations there (circ. 1599).

JOHN HOSKYNS, RICHARD MARTIN AND HUGH HOLLAND: Aubrey *(Brief Lives)* groups them as a triumvirate of friends. Their 'symposiaque excesses' are celebrated by Hoskyns in macaronic verse. The scene of the poem is laid at the Mitre, those present, besides Hoskyns, Martin and Holland, are John Donne, Henry Goodyear and Inigo Jones, all of whom were known to Jonson. (For poem, see *Hoskyns' Poems*, ed. Andrew Clark).

The traces of their relationship with Jonson are as follows:

HOSKYNS: Aubrey who knew his son, Sir Ernest, says that Jonson called him 'father' and said ''twas he that polished me.'

Lady Hoskyns (Aubrey, *Brief Lives,* under Ben Jonson) says that Jonson never writes of love, or if he does, does it not naturally.

Hoskyns, a member of the Elizabethan Academy, which was said to have revised Jonson's *Poems* and Raleigh's *History of the World* (*Shak. Eng.* I, pp. 247-248).

Hoskyns knew Sir Walter Raleigh (a friend common to Hoskyns and Jonson). 'When Sergeant Hoskyns was a prisoner in the Tower, he was Sir Walter's *Aristarchus.*' (Aubrey, *Brief Lives,* II, p. 192) Wood *(Athenae)* speaks of Jonson as beloved by Hoskyns and Martin for his classicism.

HUGH HOLLAND: Writes commendatory verses on Jonson's *Sejanus*. Writes life of Camden, Jonson's friend. Attended

Westminster School (Jonson's School) and Trinity, Cambridge. (Wood, *Athenae Oxon.* I, p. 583).

Writes verses for Sir Thos. Hawkins's translation of Horace. Sir Thos. Hawkins was a contributor to *Jonsonus Virbius.*

Holland's patroness, Lady Elizabeth Hatton, was the lady for whom Jonson wrote his *Gipsies* (Aubrey).

Holland was probably a friend of Shakespeare's; he wrote a sonnet for the first folio of Shakespeare. (*Sir Henry Wotton,* Logan Pearsall Smith).

EDWARD, EARL OF CLARENDON: He lists an early and late group of friends, both of whom are connected in various ways with Jonson. Clarendon was born in 1608; entered Middle Temple in 1625; became Lord High Chancellor of England. He was of course much younger than Jonson.

CLARENDON'S EARLY GROUP OF FRIENDS: 'Whilst he was only a student of the Law (circ. 1625) and stood at gaze and irresolute of what course of life to take, his chief acquaintances were Ben Jonson, John Selden, Charles Cotton, John Vaughan, Sir Kenelm Digby, Thomas May and Thomas Carew.' (*Autobiog. of Clarendon,* p. 8). Then follow the long and well known characterizations of Jonson and Selden.

SUPPLEMENTARY REFERENCES TO THIS EARLY GROUP OF CLARENDON'S FRIENDS:

JOHN SELDEN: When young he copied records for Sir Robert Cotton. His chamber in the Inner Temple is described — it 'looked toward the garden' and was in 'the uppermost storey where he had a little gallery to walk in' *(Aubrey).* Jonson, a great friend of Selden. Jonson says that he was 'living on his own, the law book of the judges of England, the bravest men in all languages' *(Convers.).* He had the key and command of Sir Robert Cotton's Library. John Vaughan, a member of Clarendon's early group of friends, was one of his executors.

Special references on the literary and scholarly connections between Selden and Jonson: 1605, Selden dined with Jonson and Camden *(Conversations).* 1607, Selden wrote 'Carmen Protrepticon' for Jonson's *Volpone.*

1618. Selden when called to the court for some expression of opinion in his *History of Titles* took Jonson and Edw. Heyward with him: 'being then entirely a stranger to the court and known personally there to a very few (I) was unwilling to go thither unaccompanied.' Jonson proposed to defend Selden in prison (*Castelain*, p. 935).

Selden in preparing his *Titles of Honour* refers to borrowing books from Jonson's library. Selden contributed to an unfinished *History of Henry V*, which was burned in Jonson's library. Selden probably introduced Robert Herrick to Jonson (Gosse, *17th Century Studies*).

Selden writes a letter to Jonson giving him notes drawn from the Scriptures on the counterfeiting of sexes by change of apparel (*Life of John Selden, Esq.*, Aikin). Letter dated from the Inner Temple, February 28, 1615.

Selden examined the Earl of Arundel's marbles in company with Richard James, Sir Robert Cotton's librarian and a friend of Jonson's. (Selden's *Table-Talk*, ed. S. W. Singer). This same Earl of Arundel danced in several of Jonson's Masques (*Nichols*, II, pp. 1, 174, 176, 245). Selden associated with Masque of Inns of Court (*Memoir*, G. W. Johnson). Selden on a subcommittee for dresses; Ben Jonson wrote the poetry; Inigo Jones arranged the staging; Bacon assisted Selden in arranging the dresses and devices.

Jonson's connection with Edward Heyward, Selden's friend and chamber fellow *(Table-Talk)*, is pleasant. Jonson mentions both Heyward and Selden in his commendatory verses for *Titles of Honour*. Heyward wrote commendatory verses for Jonson.

Sir Kenelm Digby: Jonson wrote verses for his birthday. Aubrey says that to Jonson he (Sir Kenelm) was a great patron. Jonson dedicated *Underwoods* to Lady Digby (Sheavyn, p. 26). Jonson's 'Eupheme,' written to Lady Venetia Digby. Sir Kenelm in 1640 compiled a second edition of Jonson's works which the author had begun in 1630 (*Greg. Smith*, p. 44).

Another general reference which emphasizes this early group of Clarendon's friends is found in *The Lives of the Friends and Contemporaries of the Lord Chancellor Clarendon*, by Lady

Theresa Lewis. She mentions among the portraits hanging together in the Chancellor's gallery, those of Jonson, Selden, Sir Kenelm Digby, Charles Cotton, John Vaughan, etc. She thus confirms the group that Clarendon has given in his *Autobiography*.

CLARENDON'S LATER GROUP OF FRIENDS: Clarendon lists a later group of friends 'in the time of his greatest business and practise.' This group includes Sir Lucius Carey, Sir Francis Wenman, Sidney Godolphin, Edmund Waller, Dr. Gilbert Sheldon, Dr. George Morley, Dr. John Earles, Mr. John Hales, Mr. William Chillingworth.

SIR LUCIUS CAREY: (Ref. in Aubrey's *Brief Lives*) 1610-1643. 'His Lordship was acquainted with the best wits of that University [Oxford] and his house was like a college of learned men.' Then follows a list of those who frequented his house, which includes Jonson. Also it seems that Sir Lucius gave the title to the *Jonsonus Virbius,* the volume of poems by divers hands in praise of Jonson: Aubrey says, "Twas his Lordship [i.e. Carey], Charles Gattaker told me, that gave the name to it' [i.e. the *Jonsonus Virbius*].

The *Jonsonus Virbius* has an eclogue on the death of Jonson, written by Falkland [i.e. Sir Lucius Carey]. This poem mentions Jonson's intended visit to him which was prevented by Jonson's death: it also gives interesting details of Jonson's method of work.

Clarendon in his *Autobiography* says of Falkland: 'Having naturally such a generosity and bounty in him that he seemed to have his estate in trust for all worthy persons who stood in want of supplies and encouragement, as Ben Jonson.' Clarendon writing of Falkland's hospitality in the country says: 'During their stay with him, he looked upon no other book except their very conversation made an appeal to some book. . . . His horse where he usually resided [Tew or Burford in Oxfordshire], being within ten or twelve miles of the University, looked like the University itself by the company that was always found there.' There was easy hospitality: 'Many came thither to study in a better air, finding all the books they could desire in his library and all the persons together whose company they could wish and not find in any other society.'

(Lives of Friends and Contemporaries of Ld. Chancellor Clarendon, Lady T. Lewis). Sir Lucius Carey married the daughter of Sir Richard Morrison. To this lady's brother, Sir Henry Morrison, Jonson addressed his 'Pindaric Ode on the Death of Sir H. Morrison.' In this poem Jonson mentions the close friendship between Sir Henry and Sir Lucius Carey and his own friendship to them both *(Underwoods, LXXXVIII).*

EDMUND WALLER and DR. GEORGE MORLEY *(Aubrey* on Waller). 1605/6-1687. 'He told me he was not acquainted with Ben Jonson (who died about 1638) but familiar with Lucius, Lord Falkland,' etc.

(Lady Theresa Lewis). She quotes the following from the Life of Waller, prefixed to *Poems of London,* 1711: 'At one of their meetings (i.e. the Town Club including Falkland, Godolphin, Wenham, Morley, etc.) they heard a noise in the street and were told a son of Ben Jonson's was arrested. They sent for him and he proved Mr. Morley, afterwards Bishop of Winchester. Mr. Waller paid the debt and this led to an intimacy between him and Morley.'

Waller contributed to both the *Jonsonus Virbius* and *The Commendatory Verses for Ben Jonson.*

George Morley told Walton of the life and last days of Jonson. Walton's account is quoted by Aubrey.

II

References showing the Relationship which Existed between Certain Prominent Scholars of the Day with whom Jonson was Connected.

WILLIAM CAMDEN, 1551-1623. Jonson's obligation to him and the story of his befriending Jonson when the latter as a boy wished to enter Westminster School is well known.

In 1600 he travelled with Sir Robert Cotton to Carlisle on antiquarian business.

In 1603 he removed on account of the plague in London to Cotton's house at Connington in Huntingdonshire. Ben Jonson was there on the same occasion *(Conversations)*.

In 1605, in his *Remaines,* he praises Jonson as of 'most pregnant wit' and worthy of the admiration of 'succeeding ages.'

He left most of his books to Cotton. For various letters between Camden and Cotton bearing on loan or gift of books, see Ellis, *Original Letters,* 2nd Series, 1827.

Camden's *Remaines* (1605) are dedicated to Sir Robert Cotton 'from my Lodgings, xii Junii, 1603. Your worship's assured M. N.'

In this work Camden says: 'If I would come to our time what a world [of poetry] could I present to you out of Sir Philip Sidney, Ed. Spenser, Samuel Daniel, Hugh Holland, Ben Johnson, Th. Campion, Mich. Drayton, George Chapman, John Marston, William Shakespeare, and other most pregnant wits of these our times, whom succeeding ages may justly admire.'

Camden was in charge of the Herald's office. Jonson was skilled in the armorial lore of his age (*Shak. Eng.,* II, p. 84) and doubtless this was another point of interest between him and Camden. (See Arthur H. Nason, *Heralds and Heraldry in Jonson's Plays*).

The first quarto of Jonson's *Cynthia's Revels* had a dedication specially printed for a gift copy to Camden. This copy is now in the Kemble Collection (P. Simpson, *Shak. Eng.,* II, p. 210).

The 1616 edition of *E. M. I.* had Camden as its patron. In this edition the dedication made to Camden in *Cynthia's Revels* is repeated (P. Simpson, *loc. cit.*).

In Jonson's Account of the Entertainment of the King in London on March 15th, 1603-4 (*Nichols*, I, p. 377), he quotes Camden's *Britannia* and calls Camden 'the glory and light of our kingdom.'

SIR ROBERT BRUCE COTTON: 1571-1631 (*D. N. B.*, Sidney Lee). He was at Westminster School where Camden was second Master.

In 1585 he took a house in Westminster, near Old Palace Yard, with a garden on the river. It was here that he had his famous library.

In 1590 he joined the Antiquarian Society. This Society, formed in 1572 for the study of English history and antiquities, included among its members Camden, Selden, Jonson, Stow, etc. (*Shak. Eng.*, I, pp. 247-248). In 1600 he travelled with Camden.

In 1603, at the time of James I's Accession, 'Bacon and Ben Jonson were often in his library. . . . When the King arrived in England the antiquary was at his country house at Connington and Ben Jonson and Camden were his guests.'

In 1610 he showed a manuscript of Camden's to Bacon.

Bacon worked up his *Life of Henry VI* in Cotton's library.

After 1605 Raleigh applied to Cotton from the Tower for the loan of manuscripts.

In 1615 he was arrested and many of his books and papers were carried to Whitehall.

In 1629 he lost his library entirely.

Sir Simon D'Ewes, in his *Autobiography*, records that on September 28th, 1624, he met Mr. John Selden at Sir Robert Cotton's house. 'Both of them being more learned than pious, I never sought after or ever attained unto any great entireness with them.'

(That Selden shared with Cotton a sincere admiration for Camden is evinced by his dedicatory verses in the 1614 edition of *Titles of Honour* to Camden, as that 'Singular glory of our Nation and light of Britain'). D'Ewes further notes in his *Autobiography* the character of RICHARD JAMES, Cotton's librarian. D'Ewes calls him 'a short, red-bearded, high-coloured fellow. . . . . an atheistical, profane scholar, but otherwise witty and moderately learned.'

This RICHARD JAMES, Cotton's librarian, was one of a family of librarians. In the records of the James family we find many traces of the literary and scholarly life of the day.

The biographical facts of Richard James's life are as follows: (See *Iter Lancastrense*, 1636. Pub. by Chetham Society and edited by Thomas Corser, 1845).

James took his M.A. at Corpus Christi in 1614.

He is characterized by Corser as 'the friend of Ben Jonson, the correspondent of Selden and Usher and Spelman and Camden and the companion and librarian of Sir Robert Cotton.'

His uncle, Dr. Thomas James, was Bodley's first librarian.

In 1624, with Patrick Young, the royal librarian, and John Selden, he examined the marbles which were in the private collection of the Earl of Arundel. (Selden in his *Table-Talk* refers to this task).

The references to scholars and authors in his letters and dedications indicates the personnel of the literary circle in which he moved.

In 1625 a Latin epistle prefacing Latin sermons has a reference to Selden.

In 1631 he wrote verses for Ben Jonson's *Staple of News*. In this year in a Latin letter to Dr. Francis James he has a long passage on Ben Jonson.

In 1630 he dedicates a collection of sermons to Sir Robert Cotton.

In 1632 his *Apologetical Essay* has dedicatory verses to Selden.

In 1633 he dedicates a collection of Latin sermons to Sir Kenelm Digby.

In 1633 he edited the Latin letters of Sir Thomas More with a dedication to Digby. He added poems on the death of Cotton and Thos. Allen, with references to Camden and Selden.

In connection with Richard James, the correspondence between his uncle, Dr. Thomas James, and Sir Thomas Bodley should be read. (See *Reliquiae Bodleianae*). There are references to Dr. Dun (sic), to Sir Walter Raleigh's gift to the Bodleian library of £50. Bodley asks if 'Mr. Dean of St. Paul's' books are in the library. There is reference to Thomas Coriat's presentation of his own book to the library. There are letters to Sir Francis Bacon, addressed as 'My good Cousin.'

SIR FRANCIS BACON: Ben Jonson celebrated his birthday (1620-21) in lines breathing of reverence and honour.

Ben Jonson in his *Timber* speaks of Bacon's oratory. Ben Jonson (Spedding, *Life and Letters of Francis Bacon*) "who had seen something of him [Bacon] off the stage, though we do not know how much, after recording his impression of the 'greatness which he could not want' . . . adds the significant and affecting remark that in the days of his [Bacon's] adversity, he 'could never condole in a word or syllable to him . . . as knowing that no accident could do harm to virtue but rather serve to make it manifest.'"

Aubrey says in reference to Bacon that 'Mr. Ben Jonson was one of his friends and acquaintance.'

In 1617 the office of Lord Chancellor of England was presented by Selden (*D. N. B.*, Selden) to Bacon on his appointment as Lord Keeper. In 1622 Selden consulted Bacon on matters pertaining to the House of Lords.

Bacon in his last will (*Memorials of Selden*, G. W. Johnson) directed that Selden's advice should be taken concerning publishing or suppressing his manuscript treatises.

Camden's only direct connection with Bacon is apparently his being summoned to Court in 1621 as king-at-arms at the creation of Bacon as Viscount St. Albans. We know that in 1610 Cotton showed a manuscript of Camden's to Bacon. Of Jonson's translation of Bacon's *Essays* into Latin see *Notes and Queries*, February 4, 1905.

JOHN STOW: 1525(?)-1605. Jonson *(Conversations)* says of Stow: 'He and I walking alone, he asked two cripples what they would have to take him to their order.' Stow in his works makes no mention of his acquaintance with Jonson.

Camden writes an undated letter to Stow bearing on the antiquities of the Abbey of Lincolnshire. Stow in his *Annales* makes a list of 'modern and present excellent poets.' In this list he includes 'M. Beniamine Iohnsō gēleman.' Stow includes among those to whom he has been especially indebted 'Sir Robert Cotton, Knight Baronet,' and 'Master Camden, Clarenceaux, King-at-arms, surnamed the learned.'

III

References to Jonson and his Group in Various Contemporary Letters.

JOHN PORY (Ellis, *Original Letters*, 2nd Series), writing to Sir Thomas Puckering, September 20, 1632, says: 'Ben Jonson (who, I thought, had been dead) hath written a play against next term called *The Magnetic Lady.*'
Pory to Sir Robert Cotton in January, 1605 (*Court and Times of James I*, T. Birch), says, referring to the masque at marriage of Essex and Frances Howard: 'Both Inigo, Ben, and the actors, men and women, did their parts with great commendation . . . . Ben Jonson turned the globe of the earth standing behind the altar.'

JOHN CHAMBERLAYNE, writing to Dudley Carleton, January 29, 1611 (*Court and Times*), records how he was sent to Cardinal Perron with a good part of Queen Elizabeth's Life, 'collected with the help of Sir Robert Cotton and written by Mr. Clarenceaux' [Camden]. Carleton in a letter to Chamberlayne (*Court and Times*) from Venice, July 9, 1613, records Lord Arundel's arrival in Italy. 'Inigo Jones [is] in his train, who will be of best use to him, by reason of his language and experience in these parts.'
Chamberlayne to Carleton, London, June 15, 1615 (*Court and Times*): 'Mr. Camden has set out *Annales*. . . . He sent me one of them yesterday which I wish you had . . . for I presume that they are well and indifferently written . . . and that they will be well received abroad.'
Chamberlayne to Carleton, London, Dec. 7, 1616 (*Court and Times*): there has been sent out of Scotland for the King's program 'all manner of furniture for a chapel which Inigo Jones tells me he has the charge of.'
Chamberlayne to Carleton (*Calendar of State Papers*, 11 May, 1622) refers to Jonson's translation of Barclay's *Argenis* at the King's request.

JOSEPH MEAD to Sir Martin Stuteville, Sept. 15, 1621 (*Baker Mss.*, vol. xxxii, p. 355), refers to Jonson's rejecting a title.

JAMES HOWELL: (*Familiar Letters*. Dates feigned but facts generally true).

After 1627 he made the acquaintance of Jonson whom he calls 'father.'

Howell to Jonson, Westminster, June 27, 1629, says he has prevented a second fire at Jonson's house. Concludes letter with 'I rest, your son and contiguous neighbor, J. H.'

Howell to Jonson, Calends of April, 1629, sends a copy of Dr. Davies' Welsh grammar to Jonson. Refers to a letter in verse which Jonson had sent him. Signs himself 'Your Son and Servitor.' (Jonson's interest in Welsh dialect is evinced as early as his *For the Honour of Wales* which was performed on Shrove Tuesday, 1617-18 or 1618-19).

Howell to Jonson, from Westminster, May 3, 1635. Recommends the 'Chatelain de Coucy' legend to Jonson's attention. He had heard the story in a coach travelling from Paris to Rouen. He says further: 'I thank you for this last *regalo* you gave me at your Museum and for the good company.' He counsels moderation in Jonson's attitude toward Inigo Jones and says 'Excuse me that I am so free with you: it is because I am in no common way of friendship.'

Howell to Jonson, from Westminster, July 3, 1635. Advises the suppression of copies of the satire on the 'Royal Architect' (i.e. Inigo Jones).

James Howell to Sir Thomas Hawkins, from Westminster, April 5, 1636. 'I was invited yesternight to a solemn supper by Ben Jonson where you were deeply remembered.' Howell explains and excuses Jonson's overpraise of himself.

IV

References Connecting Jonson with other Well-known Authors of his Day.

THOMAS CORYAT: In his edition of the *Crudities* (1611) the first set of distichs to explain the title-page are signed by Lawrence Whitaker; the second set of distichs are signed by Ben Jonson. There are also acrostic verses signed by Ben Jonson. Coryat in his Preface to the Commendatory Verses sent in by prominent literary men of the day, says that these verses have come unsolicited and that the Prince has demanded their publication. The contributors include John Donne, Richard Martin, Hugh Holland, Inigo Jones, Thomas Campion, Michael Drayton and others. In commenting on these contributions, Nichols (*Progresses and Processions*, II, p. 400) says "Ben Jonson, himself, apparently at the desire of Prince Henry, undertook to arrange that immense farrago of 'testimonies to the author's merit' which accompanied the first edition of the *Crudities*."

In the text of the *Crudities*, there is one significant reference to Jonson (p. 159 of first edition). In Venice, Coryat, hearing of the pension given to Sannazarius for being a poet, reflects: 'I would to God my poetical friend, Mr. Benjamin Johnson (sic), were so well rewarded for his poems here in England, seeing he hath made many as good verses (in my opinion) as these of Sannazarius.'

Coryates Crambe . . . . Second Course to his Crudities, printed 1611, London, by William Stansby, contains certain verses written upon his *Crudities* which should have been printed in the *Crudities*. It includes verses by Ben Jonson 'To the London Reader, on the Odcombian writer, Polytopian Thomas the Traveller.'

Coryat on his travels in the East addressed at least four letters to the Club, 'The Worshipful Fraternity of Sirenaical Gentlemen,' that met the first Friday of each month at the sign of the Mermaid in Bread Street. In his third letter to L. Whitaker (for text see *Thomas Coryat, Traveller for the English wits,* 1616) he wishes to be remembered to Ben Jonson and to have

his letter read to him.   In his fourth letter 'To the . . . Sirenaical Gentlemen,' dated 1615, he includes among those to whom he
wishes to be remembered: John Donne, Richard Martin, John
Hoskins, Benjamin Jonson, Inigo Jones and Hugh Holland.
(For comment on this letter see Gosse, *Life of Donne*, II, p. 86).

JOHN DONNE: In 1597 (Gosse, *Life and Letters of John Donne*)
probably Jonson knew Donne personally.

Jonson in *Conversations* makes two well-known comments upon
Donne: that he wrote 'all his best pieces ere he was twenty-five
years old'; that 'for not keeping of accent deserved hanging.'

In general of the relationship between Jonson and Donne, Gosse
says: 'With one great poet Donne was certainly in considerable
communication during his youth.   He was an isolated figure unlike the men round him, but so was Ben Jonson in whom Donne
evidently inspired both curiosity and respect.'   Gosse explains
how Jonson in his lost *Art of Poetry* introduced Donne as
Criticus: 'His (Jonson's) interest in Donne was genuine, and
he expressed it on occasions more responsible than his chats in
the library at Hawthornden.'   Gosse mentions Donne's Epistle
to Jonson on November 9, 1603, and quotes Jonson's Epigram
on 'Donne the delight of Phoebus and each muse.'   Jonson
sent his *Epigrams* to Donne to be revised.   Donne's 16th Elegy
was reprinted in the 1641 edition of *Underwoods*.   Of the last,
Gosse says 'Possibly it was touched up by Jonson and was
found in his handwriting among his posthumous papers.   These
are the slight and tantalizing evidences of a life-long acquaintance and esteem existing between these two great writers.   It
would be exaggeration on the documents before us, confidently
to assume that their relations amounted to intimate friendship.'
Donne's Epistle to Jonson on November 9, 1603, reveals Donne
writing 'as though (Gosse) Ben Jonson were thoroughly acquainted with the circumstances and had frankly assured the
writer of his sympathy.'

Of Donne's verses upon Jonson's *Volpone* in 1607: 'Donne ex-
tended the like indulgence to no other poet of his own or the preceding generation.   He was obviously in far closer intellectual

and artistic sympathy with Jonson than with any other professional writer' (Gosse).

In general see Gosse's *Life and Letters of John Donne* for a detailed account of the relationship between Donne and Jonson.

In the *Poems of J. D.*, issued by John Marriot, from St. Dunstan's Churchyard in 1633, Sir Lucius Carey's contribution refers to the moving power of Jonson's elegy.

SIR WALTER RALEIGH: For Jonson's connection with the *History of the World* see *Camb. Hist.* IV, p. 59; *also Proceedings of the British Academy* VIII, 30th Oct. 1918, by C. H. Firth; Gregory Smith's *Ben Jonson*, p. 31.

See 1614 edition of *History of the World* where 'The Mind of the Frontispiece to a Book' appears in Jonson's hand.

In connection with Jonson and the young Sir Walter Raleigh abroad, L. Pearsall Smith *(Life of Sir Henry Wotton)* quotes a letter from Sir Henry Wotton to Sir Ralph Winwood, dated The Hague, 1615, which records a duel fought by young Sir Walter abroad.

SIR HENRY WOTTON: It is not certain that he knew Jonson but they have many mutual associations.

It is possible that Jonson referred to Sir Henry in *The Staple of News,* in the phrase 'liegers that lie out.' (L. P. Smith, *Life and Letters of Wotton*).

Drummond says that Jonson knew Wotton's 'Character of a Happy Life' by heart. *(Conversations).*

Wotton and Jonson are listed together in Bolton's *Hypercritica* for their good writing.

Jonson's friend Hoskins and Wotton were contemporaries at Oxford. Cf. Wotton's poem on 'Sir Henry Wotton and Sergeant Hoskins riding on the way.'

In the life of Wotton by Isaak Walton *(Reliquiae Wottonianae),* Wotton's great friendship with Donne is stressed.

MICHAEL DRAYTON: (See J. P. Collier's edition of Drayton, pub. by Roxburghe Club, 1856).

Drummond *(Conversations)* says that Jonson remarked that 'Drayton feared him and he (Jonson) esteemed not of him.'

This was in 1619. The breach of feeling was healed by 1627 when first was printed Drayton's 'Vision of Ben Jonson on the Muses.'

See Ward's Diary for the episode of Drayton and Ben Jonson at Shakespeare's.

Drayton had a close connection with the Countess of Bedford who was also Jonson's friend. Drayton wrote dedicatory poem to Countess of Bedford in the first edition of 'Mortemeriados.' The 1603 edition had dedicatory sonnet by John Beaumont. The 1619 edition had verses by John Selden and Edward Heyward. Selden wrote a sonnet to 'Michael' for the 1613 edition of Drayton's poems. Selden made notes and illustrations for Drayton's *Polyolbion,* dated from 'Inner Temple, 9 May, 1612.'

SIR JOHN SUCKLING: His poetry 'Save for a few epigrammatic pieces and an imitation, written half in burlesque, of a famous song by Jonson, retains little trace of Jonson's influence.' He spoke rather scornfully of the poet's notorious boastfulness in the *Sessions of the Poets* and caricatured him with a light touch in *The Sad One.* (See A. Hamilton Thompson's edition of Suckling, 1910).

See *Session of Poets* for references to Selden, Wenman, Vaughan, Falkland, as well as Jonson. Suckling contrasts Jonson and Shakespeare in the traditional way:

> The sweat of learned Johnson's brain
> And gentle Shakespeare's easier strain.

In *The Sad One* Suckling parodies Jonson's 'Song to Charis' (Act IV), his use of stock characters in his plays, his praise of his own work. Suckling writes to Falkland on the charm of his scholarly retirement which Jonson shared. Suckling was a friend of Jack Young who by persistent tradition is reported to have paid for the carving of 'O Rare Ben Jonson' upon Jonson's grave in Westminster.

V

Jonson's Connection with Craftsmen of the Theatre

INIGO JONES: For Jonson's specific comment on his work with Jones in producing various masks see Nichols, *Progresses and Processions*, II, passim; Jonson acknowledges the share Inigo Jones had in the success of *Hymenaei*, presented on Twelfth Night, 1605-6 (Nichols, II, p. 23). He also gives Jones credit for a share of the success of the Masque for Viscount Haddington's marriage (II, p. 176) and of the Masque of Queens (II, pp. 217, 242). In general on the collaboration of Jones and Jonson see *Shakespeare's England*, II, p. 68, 328. For Jones in general see *Life*, P. Cunningham, Shakespeare Society, 1848.

For Jonson's *An Expostulation with Inigo Jones* (Cunningham, *Life*, p. 28) see Collier's *New Facts*, p. 49, which shows the text in Jonson's hand among the Bridgewater manuscripts.

For Jonson's suppression of his attack upon Jones in *A Tale of a Tub*, see Cunningham, *Life*, p. 29. For Jonson's attack on Jones in *Love's Welcome*, see Gregory Smith, *Jonson*.

HENSLOWE: For a summary of Jonson's connections with Henslowe, see *Henslowe's Diary*, ed. W. W. Greg. Pt. II, Ch. IV, p. 288.

THOS. GILES AND ALFONSO FERRABOSCO: For Jonson's connection with these musicians see Cunningham, *Life of Jones*, passim.

INDEX

Throughout the Index the initial J. stands for Ben Jonson.

his attacks, 53-57; does not express the symbolic significance of the stage until *The New Inn*, 57.

On Chapman's *Iliad*, 62; his idea of scholarship, 63 *ff.*, 81; his learning, 65; his method of handling his sources, 65, 66; insists on the spirit of learning, 67; his faith in knowledge as a cure for the Humours, 68; on the fashionable pursuit of culture, 68, 69; on the scholarly pretensions of women of fashion, 69-71; his scorn for those who make a mockery of learning, 71, 72; his friendship with Camden, 72, 73; his Epigram on him, 72; his friendship with Selden, 72-75; his admiration for Bacon, 76; R. James on his scholarship, 76, 77; on the translation of his time: Edmonds, 77, 78, Saville, 78; May, 78; and Feltham, 78; his interest in curious knowledge, 78, 79; his preference of classical to mediæval story, a matter of moral judgment, 79, 80; his theory of the function of poetry, 86, 90; animosity between Daniel attributable to opposition of their theories, 86, 87, 88; his parodies of Daniel's poems, 87; his judgment of non-dramatic poetry criticised, 88; his views on form as opposed to content of poetry, 89, 90; and Drummond of Hawthornden, 94; on amateur versifiers, 94-96; on the 'hard-headed, practical' man as an enemy of poetry, 96, 97; his sense of humour about himself, 98; in the flippant handling of lyric poetry, 98, 99.

His plays contain an interesting picture of daily life in London, 101 *ff.*, on the intimacies of domestic life, 102, 103; and the romance of trade, 103; and the life of the streets, 104, 105; music, 105, 106; puppet-shows, 107, 108; his kinship with picturesque rascals, 108, 109; on charity among the upper classes, 110; on the difference between social groups, 110-112; the foibles of society are the 'very stuff' of his comedies, 112-115.

His art compared and contrasted with that of some fellow-dramatists: Chapman, 118-125 and notes; Shakespeare, 125-127; Dekker, 127-129; Middleton, 129, 130; Marston, 130-132; his quarrel with Marston, 132 *n.*; Heywood, 132-134; Beaumont and Fletcher, 134-136; Massinger, 136, 137.

Works of, quoted or referred to:

(a) PLAYS:

Alchemist, The, 24, 26, 36, 39, 40, 41, 78, 110, 112, 113.

Bartholomew Fair, 26, 32, 33, 34, 35, 36, 41, 47, 48, 74 *n.*, 97, 103, 106, 107.

Case is Altered, The, 30, 31, 34, 51.

Cynthia's Revels, 17, 18, 19, 20, 23, 26, 30, 31, 34, 51, 52, 53, 65, 68, 69, 95, 96, 106, 110, 112, 113, 114, 122 *n.*, 132 *n.*

Devil is an Ass, The, 26, 32, 111.

Eastward Ho! (in collaboration), 132 *n.*

Epicoene, or The Silent Woman, 26, 36, 46, 51 *n.*, 70, 71, 95, 96, 104, 105, 111, 113, 114, 115.

Every Man in his Humour, 47 and *n.*, 50, 55, 72, 87, 95, 96, 97, 102, 103, 105, 108, 109, 110, 111, 112, 115.

Every Man out of his Humour, 26, 30, 31, 33, 36, 40, 49, 50 *n.*, 52, 69, 73, 80, 87, 95, 96, 105, 106, 107, 109, 112, 113, 115, 132 *n.*

Magnetic Lady, The, 33, 36, 41, 47, 68, 115.

New Inn, The, 32, 35, 57, 58, 79, 91.